Maldives

Text by Royston Ellis
Principal photographer: Marcus Wilson-Smith
Series Editor: Tony Halliday

Berlitz® POCKET GUIDE

Maldives

First Edition 2007

PHOTOGRAPHY
AFP 20; Bridgeman 17; courtesy of Anantara Resort 98; courtesy of Dhoni Mighili Resort 52, 62, 63, 66, 78, 88, 89; courtesy of Island Hideaway Resort 10, 94; courtesy of Meedhupparu Resort 55, 85; Michael Friedel/Rex Features 93; Hassan Najmy 12, 50, 68, 90; Marcus Wilson-Smith 6, 9, 14, 19, 22, 25, 26, 27, 28, 29, 30, 31, 32, 33, 34, 36, 37, 39, 41, 42, 43, 45, 46–7, 48, 54, 57, 58, 60, 64, 71, 72, 73, 74, 76, 79, 80, 81, 83, 86, 91, 96, 97, 99, 100, 101, 102, 103
Cover picture: Jack Sullivan/Alamy

CONTACTING THE EDITORS
Every effort has been made to provide accurate information in this publication, but changes are inevitable. The publisher cannot be responsible for any resulting loss, inconvenience or injury. We would appreciate it if readers would call our attention to any errors or outdated information by contacting Berlitz Publishing, PO Box 7910, London SE1 1WE, England.
Fax: (44) 20 7403 0290
Email: berlitz@apaguide.co.uk
<www.berlitzpublishing.com>

Charter a boat to drop a line: the waters of the Maldives offer some great possibilities for fishing (page 89)

For a memorable day out from your resort, visit one of the inhabited islands to see life in a Maldivian village

The minaret of the Grand Mosque in Male' (page 30)

TOP TEN ATTRACTIONS

Colourful coral and fish make the Maldives a paradise for divers and snorkellers (pages 86–9)

The island of Utheem (page 57) is the birthplace of the Maldives' national hero

Blue lagoons, white-sand beaches and fine facilities make for an island idyll at a Maldives resort

Male's National Museum (page 31) displays treasures from the days of the sultans

Where the locals do their shopping: the Local Market in Male' (page 28)

Experience the commercial hustle and bustle, Maldivian-style, of the waterfront area of Male' (page 27)

Carvings adorn Hukuru Miskiiy (page 34), a 17th-century mosque in Male'

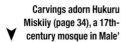

CONTENTS

INTRODUCTION

As recently as 1970, the Maldives was virtually unknown, isolated from the rest of the world by its location in the Indian Ocean, straddling the equator. Its 1,192 verdant islands, blessed with white-sand beaches and tranquil lagoons teeming with exotically coloured fish, were inhabited by poorly educated but devout, impoverished fishermen. Today celebrities flock there to relax in luxurious tropical exclusivity and the resorts host more than 600,000 delighted tourists a year.

The swift change in fortunes and fame was spearheaded by a group of adventurous Italian divers who discovered the islands for spear fishing, a practice since banned as the Maldives plays an active part in eco-conservation. From its start with two holiday islands in 1972, there are now nearly 100 resorts, each set on its own island, offering escapist dream holidays come true. The revenue from tourism, and from the organised fishing industry, has officially lifted the islands from being a UN basket case to a success story. Education is in English to university-entrance standard, there is country-wide health care, full employment, and even the remotest island has modern infrastructure.

Geography

Formerly a sultanate, the Maldives is an independent Muslim republic of small islands scattered in 26 natural atolls like a garland for 822km (511 miles) from seven degrees north to just south of the equator. Over 99 percent of its territory is

An atoll (the English word is derived from the Maldivian *atolhu*) is a large, complex ring-shaped reef structure whose islands are the tips of the broken rims of long-submerged volcanoes rising up from the ocean's depths.

sea. India lies 600km (373 miles) to the northeast, with Sri Lanka about 670km (416 miles) distant. To the west is Somalia, to the east Indonesia and Malaysia, and to the south the nearest country is the Seychelles.

Positioned at a crossroads in the Indian Ocean, the islands originally attracted seafarers, merchants and settlers from neighbouring countries, giving rise to a mixed, handsome population united by their faith (all are Sunni Muslims), and conditioned by island culture to simple self-sufficiency. Even today it seems the Maldives has not become part of the world; the world has invaded its shores.

Its small, crowded capital of Male' (pronounced Mar-lay) has narrow lanes, a fishing harbour, busy quays, a grand mosque, modern stores, teashops, restaurants and heavy traf-

Evocative Names

The Republic of the Maldives has been known by many names. In a report to the Roman Emperor Julius in 362, Ammianus Marcellinus mentions 'Divae et Serendivae, nationes Indicae', a reference to today's Maldives and Sri Lanka (known then as Serendib). The historical Buddhist chronicle of Sri Lanka, the *Mahavamsa*, tells of the first migrations of Indo-Aryans to the Maldives, calling the main island Mahiladipaka. This is Pali and means 'woman-island', perhaps referring to the island being ruled by a queen, as the Maldives was several times in its early history.

Indian traders called the islands variously Maladiv and Malodheep, both derived from the Sanskrit word for garland, perhaps because when traced out on ancient charts the chain of islands resembled a garland. Variations are the Arabic Mahal-Dheeb, from the Sanskrit Maala Dveep, which eventually became Maldives (pronounced Mol-deeves) in English. The islanders themselves never called their country anything like Maldives. In the local Dhivehi language it has always been Dhivehi Raajje (the Realm of the Dhivehin).

fic. It is home to a third of
the islands' population of
300,000. Only 198 of the
islands are inhabited, and
tourists stay on 'uninhabited' islands. This policy was
developed to allow Maldi-
vians to retain their independence and culture, and to let
tourists enjoy theirs.

Environment

The islands have neither
rivers nor hills and few of
them are more than 1m (3¼ft)
above sea level. This causes
great concern about the

**Muslim identity: minaret of the
Grand Mosque in Male'**

effect of rising sea levels, thought to be caused by global climate change. President Maumoon Abdul Gayoom was the first
statesman to raise the issue of climate change from the per-
spective of small island countries to the UN's General Assem-
bly in the 1980s, and he has been pressing his case with world
leaders ever since. The experience of the tsunami of 2004
serves as a cautionary tale. Curiously the tsunami did not do as
much damage as in Sri Lanka because it washed over islands
unopposed by landmass. However, 106 people, including
tourists, were drowned, and 12,000 people were left homeless.
Only 49 inhabited islands, mostly on the eastern rim, were
flooded, as well as 19 resorts, all since reopened.

Although visitors expect sunshine every day, it does rain
too, hence the islands' lush foliage. Weather patterns are
defined by the monsoons, with December to April being the
favourite time for tourists. The temperature rarely drops
below 25°C (77°F) and there is an average of eight hours

sunshine a day. The flora and fauna of the islands includes coconuts, breadfruit and melons; herons and geckos (no snakes); and stunningly colourful marine life.

Resorts

Tourists stay only in approved tourist resorts, on registered safari boats or in the capital, Male'. The resorts can only be reached by speedboats or *dhonis* – or by seaplane – from Male' International Airport, or by chartered safari vessels. Every resort has snorkelling, dive schools, water-sport stations, fishing, and cruises by *dhoni* to villages and uninhabited islands. They each have restaurants and bars, and most have a spa of sorts. Visitors are not allowed to bring alcohol into the country and no alcohol is permitted in Male'. However, there are bars galore in the resorts. While the resorts range in style from full-board budget accommodation to

Villas at the Island Hideaway resort on Dhonakulhi

ultra-chic luxury, they all
share the same characteristics: white-sand beach, blue
lagoon, spectacular reefs,
coconut palms, balmy sunny
days, sea-view rooms, sand
trails through flowers and
tropical glades, international
cuisine, and a swimming
pool or lagoon bathing. They
are laid out horizontally (no
lifts), so a lot of walking is
required to get from rooms
to public areas. The varied
range of resorts, from the

**Dhivehi (Dhivehi-bas,
island language) is the
southernmost Indo-
Aryan language, spoken
only in the Maldives
and in the republic's
northern neighbour, the
Indian island of Minicoy,
where it is called Mahl
or Mahal. Dhivehi has a
Sanskrit foundation and
is related to the Sinhala
spoken in Sri Lanka,
and includes other Indic
elements in it.**

new marina complex in the north to the former British air-
force base of Gan over the equator in the south, are dedicated
to providing a tranquil and fascinating holiday experience.

There are excursions to Male' that give tourists a chance to
see the Grand Mosque, the harbours, the museum and mar-
kets, to visit teashops, and to interact with local people. Maldivians are shy and respectful, and are used to fending for
themselves, exhibiting a gracious hospitality to visitors. English is a national language while Dhivehi is spoken at home.

Economy and Administration

Tourism sustains the economy (supported by fishing), and
the industry is closely regulated to maintain environmental
standards. There has been criticism from abroad that the
benefits of the tourist revenue are not reaching the entire
population, and that political freedom is limited. The government, under long-serving President Maumoon Abdul
Gayoom, recently permitted party politics and initiated dis-
cussion on changes to the constitution.

Tourism helps support demand for the traditional industrial sector of boat-building, mat-weaving, rope-making, black-smithing, handicraft-making and other cottage industries. This sector employs women and accounts for about a quarter of the workforce. The construction and tourism industries rely heavily on foreign employees.

The Maldives is developing in ways that were unimaginable even as recently as the 1990s. Over 100 more islands have been identified as suitable for tourist resorts, so the benefits of tourism revenue can spread throughout the atolls.

The 26 atolls are divided into 19 administrative units, consisting of uninhabited as well as inhabited islands, governed by an official appointed by the president as atoll chief *(Atholu Varin)*. His role is similar to that of a governor of a province. He can consult with the atoll's religious head, or *Ghaazee*, on legal matters. Every inhabited island has an island chief *(Katheeb)*, usually a distinguished island citizen appointed by the government. The 19 administrative atolls are also the constituencies of parliament and elect two members each, every five years, by universal adult suffrage. The 20th constituency and administrative unit is the country's capital, Male', which also sends two members to parliament.

Busy with the errands

A BRIEF HISTORY

The Maldives was not always the insignificant nation it was at the advent of tourism. In the Middle Ages the islands were known as the Money Islands because they were nature's mint, providing the world's trading community with the shells – cowries – that served as international currency.

The islands were formed more than 50 million years ago. Upheavals in the earth's surface resulted in the splitting of the landmass that is today's Africa and India and then the submerging of volcanoes whose broken ridges remain as the atolls. How the first inhabitants arrived is speculation, but these islands between Asia and Arabia must have been popular landfalls for ancient mariners. Historians believe there were inhabitants in the islands over 3,500 years ago. Aryan immigrants from India, probably via Sri Lanka, seem to have started settlements around 500BC.

There are ruins, many barely excavated, that indicate early settlers brought Buddhist and Hindu beliefs and architecture with them. It is logical to assume that Arab settlers would have brought Islam with them, although there is no architectural or other evidence to support this, prior to 1153 when Islam officially became the religion of the Maldives.

Legend says that even before settlers from Asia, Arabia and the ancient world arrived, there was an aboriginal race in the Maldives, the Redin, with light skin, brown hair and hooked noses. The Norwegian explorer/anthropologist Thor Heyerdahl suggested that they were sun-worshippers. In 1985 he wrote that his team 'uncovered compact mounds resembling step-pyramids, walls ornamented with script and sun symbols…'.

Islam Arrives

The legend of how the king of the Maldives embraced Islam is taught to every schoolchild. It centres around the offering in the temple one night every month of a virgin girl to appease the demon of the sea. The girl, who was chosen by drawing lots, was found dead the next morning.

Detail of Mohamed Thakurufaan's house on the island of Utheem

A visiting Moroccan trader and missionary scholar, Abul Barakaath Yoosuf, was staying at a house where the daughter was selected for the monthly sacrifice. Appalled by the custom, he disguised himself as the girl, taking her place in the temple that night. In the morning, he was found alive, reciting verses from the Holy Koran. The king asked him about Islam and was so impressed he decreed it the religion of the islands. The king subsequently became the sultan and founded the first of seven dynasties to rule the Maldives.

Invasions

The arrival of Vasco da Gama in Calicut, India, in 1498 heralded the beginning of Portuguese power in the Indian Ocean. Until then, Maldivians had lived as devout fisherfolk and maritime traders. The Portuguese attempts to control the Indian Ocean led to Male' becoming a profitable entrepôt for trading. The Portuguese wanted a share of it and coveted the Maldives because of its location and the availability of cowry shells used as trading currency, and as a convenient source of ropes, made of coconut fibre, for their ships.

Having begun a campaign of intrigue and intimidation, the Portuguese made two attempts to invade. The first attempt was defeated by Ali Rasgefaanu, who later became sultan. The Portuguese succeeded in 1558 and appointed Andrea Andreas as captain general and de-facto ruler. Resistance eventually came from the island of Utheem in Haa Alifu atoll. There, Mohamed Thakurufaan, the son of an island chief and trader, persuaded his two brothers, Ali and Hassan, to join him in fighting the Portuguese. After 15 years, he led the liberation of the islands. As sultan, he oversaw reforms to the judiciary and administration, set up a standing militia, introduced coinage (instead of cowry

Mohamed Thakurufaan

Mohamed Thakurufaan, the national hero of the Maldives, was the second of three brothers and lived in the mid-16th century on the northern island of Utheem. He was regarded as unusual even as a child because he spent days on the beach dreaming and trying to trap and tame wild birds to do his bidding. Sent by his father to India for martial arts and religious training, he returned to Utheem after four years to become captain of his father's inter-atoll trading vessel.

On his voyages around the islands he witnessed the oppression of the Portuguese occupation, including attempts to convert the islanders from Islam to Christianity. He was inspired to organise a popular revolt, and with a fast boat, *Kalhuoh Fummi*, and a small band of patriots, he developed classic guerrilla tactics of hit and run, infiltrating occupied islands at night, killing the sleeping Portuguese and then sailing away. His methods were so effective that Portuguese morale was destroyed and the governor ordered the inhabitants of Male' to accept Christianity or die. On the eve of the deadline, on the night of the 1st of Rabeeu al-Awwal in 1573, Mohamed Thakurufaan and his supporters invaded Male' and liberated the islands. The event is commemorated as National Day on the first day of the third month of the lunar calendar each year.

shells) and started trade relations with foreign countries. His reign was a period of peace and prosperity.

Having such highly prized islands flourishing through trade just off the coast of India was tempting to Indian privateers. In 1609 these Malabars descended on Male' and killed the sultan, but they were repelled. During the next four decades there were further attempts to invade by the Portuguese and by forces sent by the rajah of Cannanore. In 1650 the sultan, Ibrahim Iskandhar (1648–87), uncharacteristically went on the offensive and raided the rajah's territory, putting a stop to invasions for several years.

The Dutch began trading in the Indian Ocean and the Maldives maintained good relations with them, letting them survey the islands in 1671. There were a few more attempts to invade by Malabars from India but it was not until 1752 that one was successful. It lasted four months until the Malabars were expelled by Dhon Hassan Manikufaan, who hailed from Huraa. Huraavee Day now commemorates this victory.

The Malabars tried to invade on several other occasions. In desperation, Dhon Hassan Manikufaan made a treaty with the French, based in Pondicherry, southern India, for help in defending the Maldives. The French presence in the islands, though brief, stopped the attacks from India. In 1759 Dhon Hassan Manikufaan became the first sultan of the Huraage dynasty, which ruled, except for 1953–54, until 1968.

Stability

At the end of the 18th century, British power was becoming dominant in the Indian Ocean. Various sultans found it prudent to retain cordial relations with the British. The British were permitted to survey the islands in 1834, and British admiralty charts made then are the source of charts in use even today.

In 1887 an exchange of letters took place between the governor of Ceylon, representing Queen Victoria, and Sultan

Map of the Maldives fom 1780

Mohamed Mueenuddeen II. The motive behind this for the sultan was to keep the British – who by then virtually controlled the Indian Ocean – out of the Maldives. The relationship was uneasy but enabled the Maldives to enjoy the status of a protected state, although not officially a protectorate of Britain.

The statehood of the Maldives was recognised and Britain had no power to interfere in internal matters, controlling only external affairs. The Maldives was never a vassal state (or part) of Ceylon since the arrangement was with the governor of Ceylon as the representative of Queen Victoria.

In 1932 a written constitution was proclaimed, the islands having been governed up to then by an unwritten one. The sultan's role was similar to that of a constitutional monarch.

Sultan al-Hasan Nur ud-din Iskander II was proclaimed 'Sultan of Land and Sea, Lord of the Twelve Thousand Islands and Sultan of the Maldives' in 1935. He was forced to abdicate in 1943, creating turmoil among the islands' ruling families. In

1945 Abdul Majeed Didi was proclaimed as 'the Elect to the Throne of the State of the Maldives'. However, he remained in Egypt most of the time and was never installed as sultan.

The prime minister and effective ruler from 1945 to 1953 was Amin Didi, who became the country's first president in 1953. He is regarded as the father of the modern nation, particularly for his reform of the education system, reviving Maldivian language and literature, and giving women more of a place in society. His reforms, however, were not all popular and he was deposed and exiled to Vihamanafushi, now the resort of Kurumba *(see page 45)*, where he died in 1954.

Ibrahim Ali Didi became acting head of state from September 1953 to March 1954, when the sultanate was restored. Jala'alatul Malik Mohamed Farid I became sultan.

Independence

In 1948 Ceylon (now Sri Lanka) became independent of Great Britain, leaving the Maldives in a somewhat invidious position. The country was not completely independent because of the 1887 agreement, which was made with Britain, not Ceylon. In 1948 there was no inclination among the people or rulers of the Maldives to be independent.

That changed after the return to the status of sultanate in 1953. A young man, Ibrahim Nasir, began to make his way through the inner sanctums of power. He eventually became prime minister and negotiated independence, shaking off 'protection' from Britain in 1965. Sultan Mohamed Farid continued his role as head of state until, following a referendum on 1 April 1968, the sultanate was abolished again. The Maldives was declared a republic for the second time on 11 November 1968, with Ibrahim Nasir as president. The day is now commemorated as Republic Day. Nasir served two terms, and was succeeded as president in 1978 by Maumoon Abdul Gayoom as the result of a national referendum.

With the development of the tourist industry following President Gayoom's election and the consequent increase in foreign exchange income, the Maldives entered a period of progress. The country, which had joined the United Nations in 1965, became a member of the Commonwealth in 1982. A threat to stability occurred in 1988 when Tamil mercenaries, recruited from a terrorist group in Sri Lanka, attempted an invasion and coup. Several Maldivians were killed and Indian troops were stationed in Male' for a short period.

In 1998 a new constitution was introduced, removing many archaic anomalies and seeking to introduce a more democratic form of government. One innovation was to allow any Maldivian male seeking to become president to nominate himself for consideration by parliament.

Riots in Male' sparked off by police brutality in 2003 were followed by the re-election in November 2003 of President

Flying the flag on Jumhooree Maidan

Gayoom for a sixth term. There were more riots in Male' in 2004, with protestors demanding the president's resignation. Political reforms were announced. Elections for representatives to the Citizens' Majlis (parliament) scheduled for December 2004 were postponed because of the tsunami, which killed 106 people, flooded 49 inhabited islands and 19 resorts, and left 12,000 people homeless. The elections were held in early 2005, following which a multi-party democratic system was proposed by the government.

Democratic Reform

In March 2006 President Gayoom presented a road map for the reform agenda, designed to usher in a modern democracy. The objective was 'to secure transparency and efficiency in the management of the democratic reform agenda' and it set out various dates by which reforms were to take place. A special council with elected and appointed members was set up to revise the constitution. The first political party to be registered under new legislation in July 2005 was the opposition Maldivian Democratic Party. By the end of 2006, five groups had registered as political parties. During 2005 and 2006, political agitation intent on ousting the president took place, with street demonstrations in Male' and the arrest of participants.

Maumoon Abdul Gayoom, who was elected for his sixth five-year term as president in November 2003, was born in Male' in 1937, the tenth of his father's 25 children.

Historical Landmarks

1st century Roman manual of navigation, *Periplus Mari Erithraei*, mentions islands thought to be the Maldives.

2nd century In his *Geography*, Ptolemy mentions the Maldives.

362 A delegation from the Maldives visits Rome.

662 The king of the Maldives sends gifts to Emperor Kao-Tsung of the Tang dynasty.

1153 The king converts to Islam and becomes sultan, followed over 60 years by the adoption of Islam by all Maldivians.

1558 The Portuguese invade Maldives to monopolise trade and convert the islanders to Christianity.

1573 Mohamed Thakurufaan from Utheem leads a band of patriots and ousts the Portuguese.

1752 Malabars from India occupy Maldives for three months.

1887 An agreement gives the Maldives protection by Britain from foreign invasion.

1932 First constitution enacted under guidance from Britain.

1953 The sultanate becomes a republic for less than a year.

1965 Independence from Britain.

1968 The beginning of the Second Republic.

1972 The first tourist resort opens.

1978 Maumoon Abdul Gayoom becomes president.

1988 An invasion by Tamil mercenaries as a coup attempt is foiled.

2003 Unrest in Male' following police brutality. President Gayoom is re-elected for a sixth term in office.

2004 Riots in Male' in August result in a State of Emergency, lifted in October, and the jailing of prominent figures.

2004 A tsunami causes loss of life and extensive flooding of islands and resorts.

2005 Political parties are registered for the first time and tourism professionals join the government.

2006 President Gayoom presents a road map setting out a timetable for democratic reform, and a constitution council considers proposals.

WHERE TO GO

MALE' AND ITS ATOLL

Male', the capital, and its residential islands of Villingili and Hulhumale', and the airport island, are located in the south-eastern corner of North Male' Atoll, ideally situated for access to the resorts in both parts of the atoll.

Most visitors to the Maldives miss Male'. They are met at the airport by a resort representative and whisked away by speedboat or seaplane to their resort. Unless they are staying in Male' Atoll *(see pages 43–7)*, visiting Male' may be too far (or too expensive) a journey to make. Yet the capital gives a more realistic impression of the modern Maldives than is gained by staying in a tourist resort.

The skyline of Male', as seen on the approach to the northern inner harbour, is undergoing a rapid metamorphosis. Buildings are being torn down and replaced with 10-storey apartment blocks So urgent is the need for additional living space that a new building is used for accommodation even before it is properly finished. Male' is a city in progress.

> The apostrophe at the end of the word Male' could signify a contraction of Malei, the name of the dynasty that ruled the archipelago first as Buddhists and then as Muslims over 800 years ago.

The capital's rapid development (it looks like a miniature Singapore in the making) is the outcome of the delayed arrival of the modern world, which invaded only in the 1970s with the advent of mass tourism. As Maldivians become more sophisticated and demanding, so too does Male' itself, with air-conditioned stores

A *dhoni* moored at Male's Southern Harbour

selling electronics and fashions imported from around the world, sleek cars and motorbikes, mobile phones, cyber cafés and satellite television.

Male' has always been the political, commercial and social centre of the country, attracting residents from all the atolls. It is situated approximately in the geographical centre of the atoll chain. Its population of 100,000 includes an influx of students boarding in the town for further education, and out-islanders staying with relatives to enjoy the bright lights and attractions of the capital.

With land reclamation completed and shored up by a new sea wall, Male' has expanded to its maximum and has two overspill islands under development *(see page 40)*. Its population is crammed into an area of only 192 hectares (less than 1 sq mile). Under a project completed in 2002, its roads are no longer sand or mud but surfaced with grey tiles interlocked in a herringbone pattern. To a visitor they resemble

National Emblems

The most visible national emblem is the flag, to be seen flying every day from a huge flagpole in Jumhooree Maidan by the waterfront in Male'. The flag comprises a green rectangle with a white crescent in the centre and surrounded by a red border.

The crest of the Maldives depicts a coconut palm, representing the livelihood of the nation, a crescent and star signifying the Islamic faith and its authority, and a pair of crisscrossed national flags. The traditional title is in Dhivehi characters and translates as Ad-Dawlat Al-Mahaldhheebiyya meaning 'The State of the Maldives'.

The national tree is the coconut, known as Dhivehi Ruh, and botanically as *Cocos nucifera*. The national flower is the pink rose *(Rosa polyantha),* a popular flower with Maldivians and one easily grown in the islands. Its local name is *finifenmaa*.

pedestrian-only malls, an impression shattered by the cars that jam the main thoroughfares, queuing at traffic lights or jockeying for parking space. There are more than 12,000 vehicles registered in Male' and over 600 of them are taxis.

Getting Around Male'

To get around, the easiest but not always most comfortable way (because of the heat) is to walk. All the important sights and shops are within a few minutes' stroll of the quayside. It would take about two hours to walk the Boduthakurufaanu ring road around the whole of the

Getting around town

island, longer allowing time for stops for soft drinks and sightseeing. The walking tours by the lads who meet resort boats and guide passengers to the historical monuments take about an hour and inevitably lead to a shop selling souvenirs.

Layout

Roughly rectangular in shape, Male' is divided for administrative purpose into four wards or districts. **Henveiru** ward occupies the northeastern side, while **Maafannu** covers the northwest. **Galolhu** is the smaller ward in the centre of the island, with **Machchangolhi** ward occupying the south. Reclamation of the shallow waters within the western and southern reefs added more land to all wards, increasing the size of Male' by almost a third of its original size. The main streets lead inland from the waterfront road, known as **Bodu Thakurufaanu Magu** after the country's national hero *(see page 15)*. Opposite the quay where most resort boats land their passengers alongside the Presidential Jetty, the tourist shopping street of **Chandhanee Magu** heads inland to the south. Salesmen lurk to entice visitors to buy hand-painted T-shirts and imported, tropical island souvenirs.

One major street, **Majeedhee Magu**, bisects the town from east to west; this is lined with clothes stores, mini-supermarkets, computer centres and teashops, and is where residents do their shopping. Towards the eastern end, on the way to the artificial beach, is the National Stadium. Orchid Magu and Fareedhee Magu, which cut northeast to southwest across the formal grid pattern, and the east to west Ameer Ahmed Magu and Medhuziyaarai Magu, are the other important roads for sightseeing.

Chandhanee Magu

By the Waterfront

The quay where visitors land fronts the **Jumhooree Maidan**, a public square created in 1988, with lawns and an enormous flagpole. The stone benches placed around it provide a welcome resting place for visitors awaiting boats back to the resorts. Behind is the old, fort-like headquarters of the National Defence Force. The new headquarters is a grand, glass-fronted building on the square's eastern side.

To the west (right), facing the square, is the capital's commercial centre. Along the waterfront are warehouses or godowns. Built in the first half of the 20th century, these low and solid rectangular buildings are each a street block broad. Now they house chandlers and hardware and grocery stores that supply goods for the atoll

With its distinctive curved wooden prow, a *dhoni* is a traditional, locally made sailing craft steered by a helmsman using his foot to control the tiller. Motorised, with a speed of about 13km/h (8mph), *dhonis* are used for fishing and for carrying goods and passengers between the islands. With the addition of a deck and awning, *dhonis* are used by the holiday resorts for excursions and diving.

boats tied up at the quay in front of them. Many have been rebuilt as brightly painted glass emporia.

People fill the road in front of the **fish market** (open Sat–Thur 6am–6pm), colliding with fishermen dragging chunky tuna fish across the road from the quay to the market for gutting and selling. The best time to see the action is in

Home with the catch

the afternoon, when boats land their catch and householders rush to buy fresh fish for the evening meal. People meet to socialise amid the hubbub and then carry their fish home hanging from the handlebars of bicycles. However, even this ritual of daily life is undergoing change; at the time of writing, a new fish market was being built on the quay on land reclaimed from the sea, so the road will no longer be blocked by fishermen, vendors and shoppers.

A few blocks further westwards are the open-sided compounds where traders sell vegetables, clothes, cheap watches, firewood, and other goods that are not offered in the **Local Market** building behind it (open Sat–Thur 6am–6pm). This long, high-roofed barn is screened with green gauze and has a calm atmosphere after the frenzy of the streets around it. Stallholders display fruit and vegetables alongside neatly stacked jars of pickle and chutney, while bananas hang in bunches from the ceiling. Tourists are invited to sample local almonds and fudge-like candy, made from palm syrup. It's a popular place to take photos, and the stall-holders don't mind.

Entrance to this market is by swing doors from two side streets. The smaller gauze-screened shed on its sea-side is not for the faint-hearted since it is the dried, **smoked fish market** (open Sat–Thur 6am–6pm), the entrepôt for the product known as 'Maldive Fish'. This is considered an essential ingredient in certain curries and relishes. The salesmen cheerfully slice off a piece for prospective pur-chasers to taste.

Further westwards, along a pavement cluttered with goods overflowing from the shops beside the heavily trafficked road, is the **Atoll Post** (open Sun–Thur 8am–6pm, Sat 10am–4pm). This is the new general post office, with lots of seats inside for customers to wait until their number is called.

Next to it is a teashop, the Customs Cafeteria. The main customs building is across the road at the entrance to the dock where small cargo vessels tie up. Larger vessels an-chor in the roadstead of the outer harbour, which is defined by an imaginary triangle formed by the islands of Funadhoo, Dhoonidhoo and Vill-ingili *(see page 42)*. Cargo is ferried by lighters to the customs wharf, and on to the godowns.

Chatting at the market

Continuing westwards, the road leads to the coast and the less interesting side of Male', although it has a view of Villingili. Better to head inland and turn left into Orchid Magu, walking east towards Chandhanee Magu.

Presidential Palace

The elegant Wedgwood-blue and white building on the left is the **Presidential Palace**, called Theemuge. Beyond its wrought-iron gates the palace comprises elaborately decorated reception rooms and quiet inner sanctums with traditional furnishings. Photography is permitted from the road.

On the corner of the next block is the STO **Trade Centre** atrium, the closest Male' has to a shopping mall. The State Trading Organisation (STO) supermarket is on the ground floor with a range of imported goods and local products like tinned tuna. A branch of the Bank of Maldives is opposite, while other floors have souvenir and appliances stores. In the centre well is Café Alfresco, a day-time meeting point.

Turning right from Orchid Magu into Chandhanee Magu and walking one block leads to the showroom of the telephone company Dhiraagu and batteries of card-operated telephone booths. Beyond them, down Medhuziyaarai Magu, the entrance to Sultan's Park is marked by a roundabout on which is mounted the **Republican Monument** (Jumhooree Binaa). This abstract aluminium sculpture commemorates the 30th anniversary of the Second Republic (1998).

Islamic Centre

Grand Mosque

The golden dome of the Grand Mosque at the **Islamic Centre** (open Sat–Thur 9am–noon; free) is an eye-catching symbol of the islanders' faith. While town houses and coral-walled cottages are being replaced, the mosque and its tiered minaret remain constant. The centre is named after Mohamed Thakurufaan,

Sultan's Park

the national hero, and contains an Islamic library, a conference hall and classrooms, as well as the mosque. Its prayer hall can accommodate 5,000 and its gold dome is hollow with a white ceiling, dazzling light reflected from the shiny marble floor. It is open to visitors and while there is no entrance fee, freelance guides might solicit tips.

Sultan's Park

Gates lead to **Sultan's Park** (open Sat–Thur 8am–6pm, Fri 4–6pm), a favourite place for the young to promenade. This tranquil garden, with flowers and tropical shade trees, in the centre of the capital, is all that remains of the grounds of the Sultan's Palace.

The palace was destroyed at the beginning of the Second Republic, but one wing survived and this has become the **National Museum** (open Sat–Thur 8am–6pm; admission fee). The entrance is through the park gates to the building

Sultan's palanquin

on the right. The veranda, with its display of sandstone and coral items from excavated Buddhist temples alongside torpedoes and wooden chests, reflects the odd mix of exhibits inside.

A Dhivehi-speaking caretaker accompanies visitors up and down wooden staircases through the three floors of the old Edwardian-style building. The exhibits range from stone carvings of dragons and elephants and heads broken off Buddhist statues, to a bullet-ridden motorbike recalling the failed invasion by Tamil mercenaries in 1988.

The days of the sultans are commemorated with broad, ornately carved wooden thrones, a sultan's splendidly regal palanquin for bearing him in procession should it rain on his parade, a chest for carrying the sultan's gunpowder, a sultan's flamboyant, appliquéd umbrella, and lacquered trays for the sultan's supper. In contrast, there are coins, spiked knuckle-dusters, a stone massage bed dating from 1721, and a signed photograph of US President Franklin D. Roosevelt. Few of the items are in glass cabinets and they could be touched or picked up but for the watchful eye of the caretaker. The atmos-

The ancient mosque in the far left corner of Sultan's Park was once moved from Male' and erected on the resort island of Bandos. Then it was decided to restore it to Male', so it was dismantled, transported back, and reassembled in the park.

phere is more like an old curiosity shop than a stuffy museum and it provokes a wonderful intimacy with the past, proving to visitors that the Maldives has more to it than its tourist paradise image suggests.

Eastwards down the road are more sights of the past. An old wooden house, **Esjehi Villa**, has been converted to The Royal Garden Café, enabling visitors to contemplate its carved wooden walls and screens while sipping coffee. It is opposite the rear of the Defence Force compound and sentries peer down on passers-by from pepper-pot towers in its walls.

Hukuru Miskiiy and Medhu Ziyaarath

The chubby, white-painted round tower on the left of the road belies its age of more than three centuries. This is the **Munnaru**, a minaret dating back to 1675, used to call the faithful to prayer until 1984 when the one at the Islamic

Hukuru Miskiiy

Centre was built. It overlooks the impressive tombstones in
the cemetery in front of the **Hukuru Miskiiy** (Friday
Mosque). This mosque was built in 1656 on the site of the
country's first mosque, constructed in 1153. Its walls are
made without mortar or lime or any bonding material; its
coral blocks are bound together by hewn grooves. Coral
stones were also used for the building of its pillars, flooring
and also for some decoration. Teak, coconut timber, sandal-
wood and redwood were used for the roof, door and win-
dow frames. Inner sanctums can be glimpsed behind heavy
sliding doors and latticed screens; permission to enter is
granted to non-Muslims on application to the Supreme
Council of Islamic Affairs.

Across the road, the archway and closed blue door set
into a white wall is the entrance to **Medhu Ziyaarath**, the
tomb of Abul Barakaath Yoosuf. A plaque explains that he

Medhu Ziyaarath

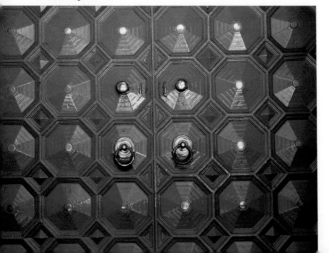

was a scholar who converted the Maldives to Islam in 1153. The tomb was called the Central Tomb both because of its location and also because of its reverence and importance over other tombs.

Sultan's Palace and People's Parliament

Behind it, the red-roofed building with fretwork friezes is **Mulee-agee**, built by a sultan in 1906 on the site of a 17th-century mansion to the design of villas in Ceylon. It was intended for the sultan's son, but the sultan was deposed and it became instead administrative offices and, in 1953, the official residence of the first president. In 1994 the Presidential Palace was built at Theemuge, and Mulee-agee was used as the president's office, until the new office was built on the waterfront.

Continuing eastwards, the road passes the **People's Majlis**, or parliament, a building donated by Pakistan. At the corner where the road joins Sosun Magu is the garden and rooftop of the Galanga Café. On the opposite corner is the office of the **National Council for Linguistics and Historical Research**, which may be visited by appointment by those interested in Maldivian culture.

More information on the history of the islands is to be found at the **National Library** (open Sat–Thur 8am–6pm), which is almost at the centre of Male', in Majeedhee Magu, opposite the Athama Palace Hotel and the inland road leading to the Central Hotel. The library contains copies of all the books published on the Maldives and is used by school-children for studying.

Down Radhebai Magu, which leads northwards from Majeedhee Magu, tucked into the corner where the road meets Neeloataru Magu, is the **tomb of Mohamed Thakur-ufaan**, the nation's hero, in the compound of the **Bihuroazu Kamanaa Miskiiy** (mosque).

Heading East

To the east of Jumhooree Maidan, where Bodu Thakuru-faanu Magu runs around the island as a ring road, the coast-guard building overlooks the harbour, with coastguard vessels anchored in front of it. The imposing building with balconies and a courtyard is the **President's Office**. The tall, polished granite-faced block next to it houses the **Bank of Maldives**. The architecture of the waterfront buildings is bright and pleasing, defining Male's modern characteristics.

The *dhonis* tied to the quayside further eastwards are the airport ferries awaiting passengers, and there is also a taxi rank. The terminal for ferries to Hulhumale' *(see page 40)* is at the northeastern corner of Male'. This is the main hotel area, with the two-storey Nasandhura Palace Hotel over-looking the waterfront, while down the lane behind it are the newer hotels Kam and Relax Inn.

Chilling out on the sea wall

The eastern coast road begins after the ferry terminal where a night carnival complex has been built, with cafés on decks raised above the sea wall and a stage for special events. There is a playing field where youths practise soccer, basketball and cricket on the sea-side, in front of the Red Zanzibar café. Here a pleasant **artificial beach** has been created on reclaimed land as Male' does not have a natural sand beach.

Tetrapod monument

This stretch of coast, with its view of the airport island, is used by residents for evening strolls. It extends to the **Tetrapod Monument** at the southeastern corner which commemorates the completion of the Male' breakwater in 1990. It also marks **Surfing Point**, where daring local boys ride the surf all day as huge waves break on the shore.

The South

Vendors sell snacks from carts at night along the boulevard of reclaimed land forming the southern waterfront. This passes by **Dharubaaruge**, the capital's conference centre, which has been the venue of major regional meetings, including two summits of the South Asian Association of Regional Cooperation (SAARC), comprising countries of the subcontinent. Its well-tended gardens add a pleasant, park-like look to this urban area of utility buildings.

Between the sea defence walls and the shore, children play in the safety of the rock swimming pool created halfway along this coast. At the end of the road the **Southern Harbour** forms the entire southwestern corner where *dhonis*, safari boats, motor launches and visiting speedboats take every available mooring and quay space. The teashops and cafés surrounding the harbour attract young people at night. Ferries for Villingili (*see page 42*) leave from a terminal at the edge of the harbour.

The ring road continues along the western coast, past the **Indira Gandhi Memorial Hospital**, donated by the government of India. Inland now, but originally offshore before the land was reclaimed, is the **tomb** marking the spot where the sultan subsequently known as **Ali the Martyr** died defending the country against the Portuguese invasion in 1558.

Hulhule Airport Island

Male' International Airport is not on Male' but on an island, Hulhule, 10 minutes away by *dhoni*. For a modern airport, it has an ancient history. The first tourist, Muslim traveller Ibn Battuta, stayed on the island during his second visit to the Maldives in 1346. In fact the island was the first holiday resort in the Maldives, as it was used by sultans when they wanted a break from life in Male'.

Hulhule is the transit point for everyone wishing to visit the resorts because resorts have sea or air connections via the island, not via Male'. For instance, someone staying on Baros in North Male' atoll wanting to visit Anantara in South Male' atoll could do so by taking a Baros transfer boat to Hulhule and there connect with the Anantara transfer boat. This costs less than chartering a speedboat for the direct resort-to-resort journey.

The British Royal Air Force, based in Gan (*see page 72*), were keen to have an airstrip near the capital which is how, in 1960, a temporary runway of perforated metal sheets was laid on Hulhule, at that time uninhabited. The first aircraft landed in October that year. A more permanent structure with a bitumen surface, built by Maldivians, was opened in 1966. For 15 years it was served by small aircraft, mostly from Sri Lanka, until the present runway was opened to long-haul flights in 1981. As well as international scheduled and chartered flights, the airport handles domestic flights by Island Aviation Services and seaplane flights of Maldivian Air Taxis and Trans-Maldivian Airways. Seaplanes depart from the lagoon at the other side of the airport and passengers have to cross the runway in special buses to check in. The seaplane departure lounge has a view of seaplanes lined up at the jetty on one side and of jumbo jets on the land runway on the other side.

The Hulhule Island Hotel can be reached by shuttle bus from the entrance to the main airport terminal. Mostly used by tourists in transit awaiting transfers to their resorts, or by business visitors to Male', it is open to non-residents. It has a

Developments on Hulhule

popular pub and a seafood speciality restaurant as well as a coffee shop. Foreigners living in Male' patronise the pub since there is no bar (and no alcohol) in Male'.

Hulhumale'

A grey-green lizard, about 20cm (8in) long, darts across the broad highway that runs around the coast of Hulhumale' island. Its presence is remarkable since at the beginning of this century the island was a lagoon where the only wildlife was fish. Now birds nest in the bushes, coconut palm trees flourish, and children play cricket in crimson-flowered scrub.

Colour, whether the sheer blue of the sky and sea, or the bleached white of reclaimed land, characterises the island. Apartment blocks have railings painted in various pastel shades, the administration building is painted an official red, the hospital roof a soothing green, and the powerhouse an electric blue. Hulhumale', however, is more than a work of art, it is the creation of visionaries concerned about the ever-increasing demand for better living conditions in the capital.

Even though the Maldives has over 900 unutilised, uninhabited islands, the government decided to build another one because the islands close to Male' (the airport island and the residential island of Villingili) had no space for expansion. Hulhumale' was created by dredging the shallow waters of Hulhule-Farukolhufushi lagoon to the northeast of the airport and 1.3km (¾ mile) from Male'. The reclamation of 188 hectares (465 acres) of land, at a cost of US$33m, was

A new industrial island, called Thilafushi, has been created in Male' Atoll out of garbage from Male' dumped on a sandbank and compounded with reclaimed land. A mosque has been built on the island and manufacturing plants and warehouses have been opened.

Hulhumale' commuters

completed in 2002. The island has been built 2m (6½ft) above sea level, making it higher than most islands in the archipelago. A highway allows vehicle access to the airport, where future expansion will add 305 hectares (754 acres). With an extension to embrace the island of **Farukolhufushi**, formerly the Club Med resort, another 204 hectares (504 acres) will be added. This is the island of the future for Maldivians.

There is a gleaming new ferry terminal building on the waterfront close to the Nasandhura Palace Hotel from which motorised passenger boats leave every 30 minutes for the 20-minute crossing to Hulhumale'. The ferry weaves its way through safari vessels moored in the shelter of the new island to land at a mirror-walled terminal. A bus waits (one fare to any destination) at the Hulhumale' terminal to take passengers to the shopping centre or apartments. Huge numbers are painted on the walls of apartment blocks for easy identification, since all blocks look alike.

Trees on Villingili

Trees have been planted along the shore, and beach-front housing lots have been staked out with survey markers. Highways have been laid with neat borders filled with plants on either side. Basic infrastructure and municipal facilities have been installed and there is a school for 400 pupils and a 50-bed hospital and a mosque for 1,500 as part of the first phase of development. By 2020 it is expected that 100,000 people will be resident on Hulhumale'.

Villingili

This island suburb of Male' has a mixed past. In 1961 a few families who lived there were moved so the island could be used as a dairy farm. A change of plan resulted in Villingili becoming a prison in 1962 and then, in 1973, a resort. Now it is an overspill residential area that tourists can visit, as many locals do when they want to picnic on the beach.

Access is by ferry from the terminal at Male's Southern Harbour. On landing, a walk along the beach heading southwards reveals a view of Male' that does seem overloaded with high-rise buildings dominating the skyline. Inland to the right is a road westwards to the residential block, while further along the shore is a *dhoni* repair yard.

There is a post office and a few basic cafés and, inevitably, given the islanders' enthusiasm for football, a football pitch. A walk around the island takes about 30 minutes and provides an opportunity to talk to Maldivians who are not in such a hurry as they are in the capital.

Male' Atoll

This atoll, officially known as Kaaf, actually consists of four geographical atolls. **Kaashidhoo**, 91km (57 miles) from Male', has only one island and about 900 inhabitants and is renowned for its toddy (a refreshing beverage made from the sap tapped from coconut trees in flower). **Gaafaru** is much larger but with only one inhabited island (also called Gaafaru), whose renown stems from being the site of half-a-dozen shipwrecks, including the 1,147-tonne iron ship *Aracan*, which foundered while sailing from Rangoon to London in 1873 and, wrecked 100 years later, the 863-ton *Lady Christine*.

The two atolls of **North** and **South Male'** make up the rest of the administrative atoll, with **Thulusdhoo** as the capital. This has become an industrial island of great importance to the economy. It began as a transshipment point for the dried, smoked and salted fish that was for

Relaxing at Kurumba

years the mainstay of the country's export trade. Now it has several warehouses, as well as garment and boat-building factories. It is the location of the bottling plant where Coca-Cola and other soft drinks are produced using water converted from the sea, resulting in a great saving on foreign exchange. Tourists can visit the island by chartered *dhoni* from Male'.

There are only a few inhabited islands in the whole atoll, since Male' itself has become home to a third of the country's population. More than half of the 72 uninhabited islands in the atoll have been transformed into tourist resorts. **Dhoonidhoo** (west of the airport) is classed as uninhabited but tourists are unlikely to want to stay there – it is the prison island. Until 1964 it was the official residence of the British representative whenever he visited the Maldives.

Visiting Resorts from Male'

There are a few resorts within a 15-minute speedboat ride from Male' that welcome visitors who are not their guests. Permission in advance needs to be obtained from the management before visiting any resort.

Kurumba Maldives is the most popular resort open to non-residents because of its seven top-class restaurants. The resort can be visited during the day, which gives a chance (for a fee) to laze on the beach and enjoy its facilities. Its sister resort, Full Moon Maldives, which has Thai and Mediterranean restaurants, can also be visited from Male'.

Less formal in its approach to visitors is Bandos, which has become accustomed to people popping over from Male' for the day, especially on Fridays. The island's management also run Kuda Bandos, its tiny satellite, as a picnic island equipped with changing rooms, and this can be leased for the day by groups. On Fridays Kuda Bandos is reserved for Maldivians and resident foreigners who travel by special *dhoni*, leaving Male' from Jetty No. 7 at 8.30am for the 45-minute journey.

Furnishings at Baros

The first holiday resorts in the Maldives, Kurumba and Bandos, were opened in 1972 in Male' Atoll, on islands only 20 minutes by *dhoni* from the capital. **Kurumba**, originally called Vihamanaafushi, is where Mohammed Amin Didi, the first president of the Maldives, was exiled. He was buried there in January 1954. Over the years, the resort has been transformed several times so that it remains the leading resort in grandeur and quality, as well as longevity.

Bandos bore the name Bodubados until becoming popular as a resort. It has a smaller sister island neighbour, Kuda (little) Bandos, open to the public on Fridays and by permission to visitors on other days of the week. **Baros**, to the centre of the atoll, is also one of the pioneer resorts, having opened in 1973. It specialises in luxury diving, as well as luxury accommodation.

The highest concentration of resorts, including many of the leading ones, is in the northern part of Male' Atoll. One is the glitzy **Paradise Island**, 20 minutes from Male' by speedboat, which has the big-city ambience of glamour and glitter: a conference hall with the latest gadgetry for presentations, several ever-open bars and a speciality restaurant at both ends of this long island.

The ultra-exclusive resort of **Soneva Gili** was the first all-water villa resort in the Maldives, and on approach by sea its wooden cabins seem to be sprouting from the lagoon bed. Other luxury resorts include **Four Seasons** at Kuda Huraa, **Banyan Tree** at Vabbinfaru, **One & Only Reethi Rah**, and the incredible **Huvafenfushi** with its elaborate overwater accommodation and spectacular underwater spa.

At the opposite end of the accommodation spectrum is tiny **Giraavaru**, on the western rim. A basic resort popular with independent, low-budget travellers, the island is said to be home to descendants of the Maldives' aboriginal inhabitants, but some experts like H. C. P. Bell *(see page 51)* believe those inhabitants descended from early Dravidian settlers.

South Male' Atoll

It takes about 10 minutes by speedboat to cross the Vadhoo Kandu, some 4km (2½ miles) to **South Male' Atoll**. In ancient times this was called Biyaidhuvu Atoll, which suggests that the

Banyan Tree Resort

island in the centre known as **Biyadhoo**, now a resort, may once have been the most important one in the atoll. Now **Guraidhoo** has that distinction as it is the most populous. The 2004 tsunami affected the eastern edge of the atoll. Seven resorts closed, but they have now re-emerged after a refit. Among them is the resort formerly known as Dhigufinholhu, with sister islands of Bodu Huraa and Veliganda Huraa. It reopened in late 2006 as **Anantara**, changing image to become an up-market resort with a distinct Thai touch. Indian influence is also in the atoll, with the **Taj Exotica** resort at Embudhu Finolhu. There are 15 resorts in the atoll, and nine inhabited islands.

Almost there – new arrivals at a resort

NORTHERN ATOLLS

There are seven atolls to the north of Male' Atoll. Although a couple of uninhabited islands opened there as resorts in the 1980s, the northern atolls have only recently become easily accessible to tourists. Even in the mid-1990s, those two resorts, now known as Soneva Fushi (Kunfunadhoo) in Baa Atoll and Kuredu (Kuredhdhoo) in Lhaviyani Atoll, could only be reached after a long journey by boat. Access to the resorts in the northern atolls is now by seaplane or fixed-wing aircraft.

For passengers of planes flying northwards from Male', a wonderful view of the northern atolls unfolds: a scintillating seascape of round, forested islands with wraparound white-sand beaches. The inhabited islands can be easily pinpointed by the communications towers rising from the centre of them, and by squares cleared among the coconut palms for football pitches.

Baa Atoll

Baa Atoll is the closest to Male' Atoll. Its thriving capital, **Eydhafushi,** with busy harbour, is 64 nautical miles from Male'. It is one of the islands visited by tourists staying in the atoll's resorts of Soneva Fushi, Royal Island (Horubadhoo), Kihaadhuffaru, Reethi Beach and the new Four Seasons at Landaa Giraavaru. Eydhafushi is typical of an inhabited island that has developed through income from islanders working in the tourist and fishing industries, and in a way resembles a miniature Male' – a bit of a disappointment for tourists seeking a typical tropical island.

That is to be found across the atoll, near the resort island of **Coco Palm** (Dhunikulhu) at **Thulhaadhoo**. This island is famed for its lacquer work, although fishing is its main industry and its sandy lanes are deserted during the day when most of the men are at sea. The lacquer workers create vases and chesspieces from wood on ancient lathes. These objects are lacquered using a traditional method with the distinctive colours of black, yellow and red with hoops, scrolls and flourishes. Pieces are much sought after as souvenirs, but since they are pre-sold and made on assignment by the craftsmen of Thulhaadhoo, it is difficult to buy them on the island. The posts supporting the roof of the island's open-sided *hulhu-ashi* (community shelter), where the islanders relax in the heat of the day, are lacquered.

Every island in the Maldives has a name, usually a very old one. Many islands have the same name and so are identified according to which atoll they belong. Most names end in variations of 'dhoo' or 'fushi', both meaning 'island' in Dhivehi.

Islands that include the word 'huraa' in the name are rocky ones, while a name with the word 'finolhu' indicates a sandy island that is lacking in heavy, established vegetation.

Just south of Baa Atoll is a mini atoll with three inhabited islands which were home to exiles from Male' during political upheavals in the 1960s. The island of **Goidhoo** was invaded by 4 million flying fish in 1963. Another island, **Fulhadhoo**, is where the French explorer Francois Pyrard *(see opposite)* was shipwrecked and captured in 1602, remaining for several years before escaping and writing a swashbuckling history of the islands and his escapades.

In Baa Atoll, north of the Royal Palm Resort, is the island of **Kihaadhoo** where village women can be seen making wickerwork items such as food covers and containers. These are sold direct to resorts to be converted into items of island décor, like novel lamp-shades, not as souvenirs; an example of how the tourism industry is keeping a dying craft, and the villagers, alive.

Local crafts live on

The oldest resort in the atoll, now known as **Soneva Fushi**, is rare in the Maldives for its size (a strip 1.5km/1 mile long) and natural vegetation. Accommodation is in lavish timbered villas, kitted out with trendy designer accessories, each villa set in a plot of wilderness by the beach. A devotion to ecological-correctness prevails, but with all creature comforts. The resort offers full-day trips to some of the 30 dive sites identified in the atoll.

Four Seasons Resort Maldives at **Landaa Giraavaru** is the atoll's newest and occupies the entire 18-hectare (44-acre) island, a natural wonder with its western tip sloping into a 2-km (1½-mile) lagoon and surrounded by white sand beaches. The Maldives' first 'Ornamental Fish Breeding Programme' to breed anemone fish (clown fish) has been set up on the resort. The goal is to prevent depletion of fish in the wild by providing an alternative supply for the aquarium trade. The programme also provides a source of income for the atoll inhabitants as proceeds from sales stay within the community.

Some of the 50 uninhabited islands in Baa Atoll, their vegetation untouched and their beaches rarely trodden, are used

Shipwrecked Visitors

In 1602, the vessel *Corbin*, one of the first two French vessels to voyage to the East, was shipwrecked on Fulhadhoo. One of the survivors, the ship's purser, Francois Pyrard of Laval, wrote a swashbuckling account of his enforced five-year stay in the islands. He noted the impact of the Portuguese and the independent spirit of the islanders. The account was published in French in 1611 and an English translation, by two British authorities on the Maldives, Albert Grey and H.C.P. Bell, appeared in 1887.

H.C.P. Bell, then in the Ceylon Civil Service, was himself shipwrecked in the islands in 1879 and used the opportunity to write a report for the Ceylon Government. His second visit was in 1920 after he had retired as the Archaeological Commissioner of Ceylon and this was followed by a stay of seven months in 1922. Bell not only investigated the Buddhist ruins in the islands, he was also granted access to and copied ancient historical records written in Dhivehi. His *Monograph on the History, Archaeology and Epigraphy on the Maldive Islands* was published in 1940, introducing the unique culture of the Maldives to the world.

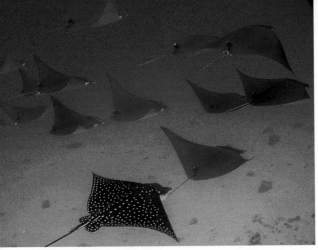

Migrating mantas off Baa Atoll

for excursions by the neighbouring resorts. The reefs are in
pristine condition, and the unspoilt natural beauty of the atoll
is readily apparent to divers and snorkellers. Large numbers
of mantas and whale sharks visit the atoll during the southwest monsoon, especially from May to July.

Lhaviyani Atoll

To the west is Baa's twin, **Lhaviyani Atoll**, with over 50 uninhabited islands and only four residential ones. The capital
is **Naifaru**, which has a branch of the Bank of Maldives and
a powerhouse supplied by Japan. The island of Naifaru used
to be renowned for the skills of some of its inhabitants in
indigenous medicine.

Many of the residents now work in the modern tuna-canning
factory on the nearby uninhabited island of **Felivaru**. This is
the only canning factory in the country and produces about
90,000 tonnes of tinned tuna per year and employs 2,000 staff.

Tuna is caught using the pole-and-line method, thus encouraging a sustainable, environment-friendly fishing industry.

Unusually, most of the islands – which are large with dense vegetation – are situated on the outer rim of the atoll. The atoll boasts a dive site known as 'the boatyard' which offers divers the unique opportunity of enjoying two wrecks in one dive. Lhaviyani Atoll is home to about 8,000 people.

One of the earliest resorts in the Maldives (opened in 1978) is **Kuredu**, at the northern tip of the atoll. This was originally a camping resort with just 48 beds. Now it has spread throughout the island (which has over 3km/2 miles of beach) and has accommodation for 660 guests and a golf course. There are 40 dive sites within boat distance, although the resort offers lots to do on shore and has a reputation as an all-inclusive party island.

Three resorts opened 21 years after tourism first came to the atoll are **Komandoo Island**, the triangular-shaped **Palm Beach** (Madhiriguraidhoo) and **One & Only Kanuhura**.

Raa Atoll

The large **Raa Atoll**, with 90 islands and a population of some 12,500 in 16 of them, lies to the east. It is actually two natural atolls, combined for administrative purposes, and measures 65km (40 miles) from north to south, and 28km (17 miles) from east to west.

Close to its outer, eastern rim is **Kadholhudhoo.** Over 3,000 people live in this island of 12 hectares (30 acres). Overcrowding is due to its proximity to bountiful fishing grounds and, with its narrow alleys, clusters of squat, coral cottages, and lack of beaches, it bares little relation to an idyllic tropical island. Fish caught and dried here is sent to the industrial complex at Thulusdhoo *(see page 43)*.

The atoll's capital, which houses the regional hospital, is **Ugoofaaru**. The largest fishing fleet in the Maldives is based here. North of it is **Rasgatheemu** which, according to legend, is where a princess and her consort, exiled from Sri Lanka, landed and began a dynasty long before the advent of Islam. Villagers claim a dip in the ground used to be a king's cave. Houses are in their own coral-walled compounds where breadfruit and oleander flowers can be seen growing as smoke billows from coral chimneys and fish is cured.

Another island where visitors are welcomed is **Alifushi** at the atoll's northern tip. The flourishing boat-building industry there was begun by local carpenters and developed into a government-sponsored boatyard opened in 1983. *Dhonis* adapted from traditional style for motorised fishing are built from imported timber and sold on time-payment terms, thus encouraging both fishermen and boat builders. Toddy from Alifushi is refreshing when drunk early in the morning before fermentation begins.

Boat building at Alifushi

Visits to these inhabited islands and to uninhabited 'picnic' islands can be made from the atoll's sole resort, **Meedhupparu**. This large island was in 2006 reborn with the brand name of Adaaran. As well as over 200 rooms built in close proximity to each other and 20 luxurious water suites linked by wooden jetty, the resort has an ayurveda vil-

Meedhupparu diving

lage where guests experience traditional Sri Lankan herbal therapy. It is reached by seaplane and offers an all-inclusive holiday with organised group activities.

Noonu Atoll

To the west, **Noonu Atoll** is being developed with two resorts, **Maavelavaru** and **Randheli**, which will be bases for visitors to explore this tranquil atoll. It shares the geographical atoll of Miladhunmadulu with its neighbour, Shaviyani Atoll. Noonu Atoll comprises 14 inhabited and 60 uninhabited islands and is known for its fishing and yams. **Manadhoo** is its capital, while **Velidhoo**, easily reached from Randheli, has links with tourism through the safari boats that are made and repaired there.

Shaviyani Atoll

Shaviyani Atoll has several islands of interest to visitors, who will be able to visit them when the resort being developed at **Dholhiyadhoo** is in operation. The island of **Narudhoo** has some picturesque inland lakes, while **Kaditheemu** has historical relics, including the doorframe of the mosque on which is carved the oldest-known written Thaana script, which dates the original mosque to the 16th century. Thaana is the old version of the present-day script used for writing Dhivehi.

Feevah has a 17th-century mosque and is known for its production of jaggery (a fudge-like confection made from syrup produced from toddy extracted from the coconut palm). **Maakadhoodhoo**, the most populated island in the atoll, also produces this coconut-palm candy. The uninhabited island of **Nalandhoo** is associated with Mohamed Thakurufaan, the national hero of the Maldives, who hid his fast sailing boat, *Kalhuoh Fummi (see page 15),* in a creek there while being chased by the Portuguese.

Thiladhunmathi Atoll

Forming the southern part of the natural atoll of Thiladhunmathi, **Haa Dhaal Atoll** has one of the most developed islands in the north, **Kulhudhuffushi**. Its inhabitants are renowned for being strong and hardworking, hence they are in demand in the construction industry and as seamen. Their income has helped develop the island with modern buildings and it is home to the Northern Regional Hospital and Northern Secondary School. **Faridhoo**, in the centre of the atoll with about 100 inhabitants, lies 2.5m (8ft) above sea level, making it one of the highest islands in the Maldives.

There is a domestic airport on the island of **Hanimaadhoo** in the north of the atoll that gives access to the resorts in the area. Hanimaadhoo has a good anchorage and there is a jetty within walking distance of the airport for transfer of passengers to resorts. The island, with over 500 inhabitants, is well developed, with cars, paved roads and a horticultural project based on hydroponics.

The airport, which is the most northerly in the country, has a recently upgraded runway equipped for night landings. While its terminal is small, there is an airport café opposite where a

24-hour taxi service is advertised. Served by the Dorniers and Dash-8s of Island Aviation Services, it is seeing an increased number of flights as new resorts open in the area.

The first of these new resorts is Island Hideaway, on Dhonakulhi Island in **Haa Alif Atoll**, the administrative northern half of Thiladhunmathi Atoll. Alidhoo and Hodaa-fushi are other resorts being developed. Guests staying in this atoll can visit islands that are known to all Maldivians because of the part they played in the country's history. In the centre is **Utheem**, the birthplace of Mohamed Thakurufaan, who liberated the islands from Portuguese rule *(see page 15)*.

Visiting Utheem is a unique experience, not only because of its historical connection but also because there is more to see than on other village islands. Until the planned jetty is built, visitors have to wade ashore like the inhabitants

Mohamed Thakurufaan's house on Utheem

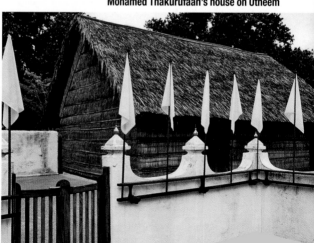

School artwork on Utheem

have always done. A broad avenue of sand leads from the beach to a grand, gnarled tree protected by a wall and known as the Sea Trumpet Tree *(Cordia subcordata)*. The tree is said to have grown from a thick branch planted by Mohamed Thakurufaan to repair his weaving loom, and it can indeed be dated to the time of his youth – the early 1540s. Weaving was an established industry in the Maldives during ancient times.

The **Bodu Thakurufaan Memorial Centre** (open Sat–Thur; admission fee), completed in 1986, flanks a square of sand and shade trees lined with the reclining, coir-webbed chairs called *joli*. The building shares the square with a school on the left and a library on the right.

About 100 paces away is the highlight, the cottage of wooden panels and sliding doors where Mohamed Thakurufaan was born and brought up. Walls bedecked with white flags surround it. The low building has been raised from its original height for easier access and the thatched roof has been replaced with a composition roof, perhaps more suited to a resort bedroom than a building dating back 450 years. A guide shows visitors around, explaining about items of furniture and describing the hero's exploits. Afterwards visitors are taken to the ancient mosque where Mohamed Thakurufaan worshipped and where his father is buried.

Other islands in the atoll connected with Thakurufaan are Baarah and Thakandhoo. **Baarah** is a crescent-shaped island that was an outpost of the Portuguese occupation, and it is said that some inhabitants have inherited Portuguese features with the girls of Baarah renowned for their beauty. It was on Baarah that Mohamed Thakurufaan built his fast sailing boat, *Kalhuoh Fummi*.

The island of **Thakandhoo**, on the opposite side of the atoll, has the tomb of the eldest Thakurufaan brother, Ali, who died while trying to rescue his wife, who was a hostage of the Portuguese. **Kelaa**, at the northern tip of the natural atoll, was a British base from 1934 until the end of World War II. With just under 1,000 inhabitants it has become developed and the traditional thatched houses with sliding wooden doors have mostly disappeared.

The resort of **Island Hideaway** at **Dhonakulhi** is not only the northernmost resort but also the only marina in the Maldives. Few yachts have yet found their way there since the marina opened in 2005, although there are berths for 25 vessels, with full bunkering facilities. Yachts, which must first be cleared by the authorities in Male', are welcome and their

Ancient Proverbs

These ancient proverbs, translated from Dhivehi but with much the same meaning in English, give an unexpected insight into matters of greatest concern to the islanders.

'Like pouring water into a broken pot.'

'The water pot that is full will not shake.'

'The cooking pot may be bad but the rice boiled therein good.'

'Pots get broken by the man using them.'

'Large was the fish that escaped.'

'Coconut can be eaten only when you have teeth.'

'Collect water while it rains.'

'Two swords cannot be kept in one scabbard.'

guests can use the resort's bars, restaurants, spa and cyber centre. The island gives an idea of how Maldivians used to live, since only 5 percent of its 234,000 sq m (280,000 sq yds) with 1.4km (about 1 mile) of beach, has been developed. Sand trails through the jungle link just 43 thatched-roofed villas, each of which is situated in its own secluded forest glade by the beach. An *undolhi* (Maldivian swing seat) in every garden is typical of the way islanders relax, although the individual villa swimming and plunge pools are a distinctly modern touch.

Children love to explore the trails (bicycles are provided) and there are special supervised activities for them, as well as a children's club. Adults are cared for by young Maldivian butlers, with one assigned to every villa, who meet guests on arrival at Hanidmaadhoo airport and tend to their needs. The staff slogan is: 'The answer is Yes; what's the question?'

Sea view at Dhonakhuli Island Hideaway Resort

Ihavandhippolhu

To the north of Dhonakulhi, the natural atoll known as **Iha-vandhippolhu** completes the northern atolls. The northern-most inhabited island of the Maldives is **Thuraakanu**. About 200 people live on the island and there is little for visitors to see; landing is difficult because of the swells and absence of a lagoon. India is about 590km (377 miles) to the northeast.

SOUTHERN ATOLLS

South of Baa Atoll and parallel to the southern part of Male' Atoll are the atolls of Rasdhoo and Ari (also known as Alif). In the 1980s there were six resorts; now there are 30, including Dhoni Mighili, billed as a 'picnic island'.

The opening of the other southern atolls to tourists has only begun in recent years, as the policy of sharing the revenue and employment that tourism brings is developed. Many of the islands that in 2006 were put up by the government for bidding as future tourist resorts, are located in the southern atolls.

Physically and climatically the atolls are like their northern sisters, although the people are, perhaps, shyer since they have not had so much interaction with tourists. The exception is Addu (Seenu) Atoll across the equator where the British presence and influence from 1941 to 1976 is still remembered.

Rasdhoo Atoll

The island of **Kuramathi** in **Rasdhoo Atoll**, administratively part of Ari Atoll, was opened as a resort in 1977 and, being long and with tropical vegetation giving privacy to the accommodation units, has become three separate resorts: **Village**, **Cottage** and **Blue Lagoon**. Safari boats bring visitors to the islands, their passengers often dropping in to Kuramathi Village, where the atmosphere is lively. The neighbouring inhabited island of Rasdhoo – where guests go to see village life – is 10 minutes away by *dhoni*.

North of it lies **Thoddoo**, an island with a secret history. In 1958 a Roman coin dated to 90BC was found there, pre-dating the earliest 1st-century AD reference to the islands in a Roman manual of navigation. The ruins of a Buddhist temple can still be seen and a huge statue of Buddha was found hidden in a chamber, together with other relics. The island is known to Maldivians as the source of delicious watermelons.

Ari Atoll

Ari (or Alif) **Atoll** extends for 76.5km (48 miles) from north to south and is 28km (17 miles) across at its widest point. Only 18 islands are inhabited and Rasdhoo was the atoll's capital before Mahibadhoo, a more industrial island on the southeastern rim of Ari Atoll, became the administrative headquarters. From Male' International Airport resorts can be reached by speedboat (about a 90-minute journey) or by seaplane. The

A diver's paradise

atoll has some exceptionally exciting dive sites, including the hammerhead point in Rasdhoo Atoll; Maaya Thila in northern Ari Atoll, which is a protected site; and places in the south famous for sightings of whale sharks.

Guests at **W Retreat & Spa**, which has taken over the island of **Fesdu** in the centre of the atoll, are encouraged to visit islands with ancient monuments in Faafu Atoll *(see page 65)* and Laamu Atoll *(see page 67).*

Jetty at Dhoni Mighili

Employing staff from 28 countries, this resort has a cosmopolitan atmosphere. The interiors of its 78 private retreats are designed like slick city apartments but with plunge pools amid the bougainvillaea by the sea. The resort, which opened in 2006, has enough organised activities and outlets to make it a destination in itself. If walking around this small island gets too enervating, there are complimentary self-service cool soft drinks and ice-cream stations every few metres.

In complete contrast to the urbanity of Fesdu, and only 10 minutes westwards by speedboat, is the tropical rusticity of **Dhoni Mighili**. With a sand-floored pavilion as reception, bar and restaurant, and a private motorised sail *dhoni* for every two of its 12 guests, the island is a good base for touring the atoll. Five uninhabited islands and three sandbanks within short cruising distance make it possible to enjoy a pampered castaway life on them as well.

The two main islands in the atoll with appeal to visitors are Mahibadhoo and Dhangethi. Guests at **Mahibadhoo** land at a

Great blue heron

pretty wooden archway, and there are some brightly painted village houses to see. As well as being the capital, Mahibadhoo is the location of a hospital and the Atoll Educational Centre, which educates children from regional schools up to university entrance standard. Over 2,000 people live there and reef fishing is the main occupation, although the men have branched out into building *dhoni*s for diving. At **Dhangethi** there is a Cultural Centre and Museum (open by appointment; admission fee). Exhibits portraying village life are on display and there are reconstructions of typical village buildings, such as the residence of the island chief and a fisherman's house, open to visitors. Villagers demonstrate the traditional arts of thatch-making, weaving and boat building. A lunch of local dishes can be arranged.

In the deep south of Ari Atoll, the islands of Maamagili and Fenfushi are a source of sand and coral for building.

Vaavu Atoll

The next four atolls to the south form a parallelogram with Vaavu and Meemu on the eastern side and Faafu and Dhaalu on the west. **Vaavu Atoll** is the least-populated atoll with only five inhabited islands, and two resorts, both popular with Italian guests for water sports and diving.

The atoll actually comprises two geographical atolls; the main Vaavu Atoll and large circular **Vattaru Atoll**, to its south, consisting of just one uninhabited island. Vaavu is a boot-shaped atoll with the island of **Foththeyobodufushi** (previously two separate islands but now joined by sand) at the toe being the easternmost land point of the Maldives. An unbroken reef stretches 55km (34 miles) across the base of the atoll.

Vaavu Atoll has been exposed to tourism since 1975 but remains isolated and less commercialised than other tourist atolls. It is much visited by safari cruises and considered to have the best dive site in the country and one of the top five in the world. There are about 17 islands in the atoll in addition to several small islets.

Meemu Atoll

Its southern neighbour, **Meemu Atoll**, has lots of isles and islets on its rim but none within the atoll. There are nine inhabited islands and the capital is Muli. The atoll is a port of call for vessels plying between the southern atolls and Male', with boats stopping over for the night at Muli. There are two resorts, reached by a 40-minute seaplane flight.

Faafu Atoll

The nearly circular **Faafu Atoll** is at the northwestern tip of the parallelogram and has only five inhabited islands and one resort. At its southwestern edge lies the island of **Nilandhoo**, which

In Meemu Atoll there is an inhabited island called Kolhuvaariyaafushi, known for its yams. The chief mosque is on the site of an earlier one, which was built of wood from the remains of *Kalhuoh Fummi*, the fast sailing boat used by Mohamed Thakurufaan. The national hero's sword, measuring 62cm (24½in) long, was deposited in that ancient mosque.

boasts evidence of a past that embraces the main religions of the Indian subcontinent. A mosque, 800 years old, built with stones from a Hindu temple, has ornate stone carvings and ornamental wooden scroll work. A Hindu complex on the island was unearthed by the Norwegian explorer/anthropologist, Thor Heyerdahl, who identified its friezes as being from pre-Islamic Buddhist temples.

Dhaalu Atoll

Faafu's southern neighbour, similar in shape, is **Dhaalu Atoll**. The country's finest gold- and silversmiths are reputed to come from this atoll, following a tradition begun when an ancient sultan's goldsmith was exiled to the atoll. The islands of **Ribudhoo** in the centre and **Hulhudheli** on the western rim have jewellery makers. There are eight inhabited islands; **Kudahubadhoo**, at the atoll's southern tip, is the capital.

Loggerhead turtle

Meedhoo is a village island popular with guests staying on the atoll's two resorts, Vilu Reef and Velavaru Island, about 15 minutes' *dhoni* ride away. It takes about 45 minutes by seaplane to get to the resorts from Male'.

Thaa Atoll

Thaa Atoll lies at the end of the parallelogram of atolls. It is almost circular (38km/24 miles long by 47km/29 miles wide) and has a reputation for good fishing. Other local trades are mat-weaving done by women on the island of **Buruni** and carpentry by the men of **Kadoodhoo**. **Dhiyamigili**, on the eastern rim, has traces of the home of the founder of the Dhiyamigili dynasty of sultans that ruled in the 18th century.

There are 13 inhabited islands in the atoll. One of the longest uninhabited islands in the archipelago, **Kalhufaha-lafushi**, is on its eastern rim. This began as three islands, Kalhufaraa, Fahala and Rakeefushi, and has been allocated for development as a resort, the first in the atoll.

Laamu Atoll

The next southern atoll, Laamu, is served by a domestic airport at **Kadhdhoo**, and is approximately halfway between Male' and Addu, the southernmost atoll in the archipelago. Once an important religious centre and regional power base, it is, after many quiet centuries, likely to regain importance as tourist resorts open in the area. The atoll has 12 inhabited islands and over 70 uninhabited ones set in its horseshoe shape. Its islands of **Gamu** (Gan) and the capital, **Fonadhoo**, are both large and support three villages on each.

The atoll has plenty of relics of the past. **Isdhoo** island has a mosque over 300 years old, with many calligraphic flourishes in its stonework, hand-carved rafters and lacquered pillars. **Gaadhoo**, at the southern tip, has ruins that were probably once part of a huge Buddhist stupa (dome).

Huvadhu mat-maker

Huvadhu Atoll

Huvadhu Kandu or One and a Half Degree Channel, the largest gap of ocean in the Maldives between two atolls, separates Laamu from its southern neighbour, Huvadhu Atoll. **Huvadhu Atoll** is divided into Gaaf Alif (North Huvadhu) Atoll and Gaaf Dhaal (South Huvadhu) Atoll. It is the world's largest atoll, with a lagoon area of 2,237 sq km (864 sq miles).

Gaaf Alif has 10 inhabited islands and over 80 uninhabited ones, many of which have ruins of ancient Buddhist stupas. The people of the capital, **Viligili**, are renowned mat-makers, while the inhabitants of **Dhevvadhoo**, in the centre, are good at textile-weaving and coir-making.

Gaaf Dhaal has more than 150 uninhabited islands, as well as seven inhabited ones with populations of over 1,000. More than 6,000 people live in the capital, **Thinadhoo**, which is situated on the atoll's western rim and is served by the domestic airport built nearby on the uninhabited island of **Kaadedhdhoo.**

On the southern rim, the islands of **Gan** and **Vaadhoo** have ruins from an earlier Buddhist civilisation. Vaadhoo also boasts a 17th-century mosque. Two small inhabited islands, **Fares** and **Maathoda**, close to the equator, were joined by a causeway in 1981.

Gnaviyani Atoll

The largest (4.4km/2¾ miles by 2.8km/1¾ miles) single island in the Maldives constitutes **Gnaviyani Atoll**, the only administrative atoll with a solitary island, also known as Fua-Mulah Atoll. The island is called variously **Foammulah**, Fua Mulaku and Fuvah Mulah. It lies south of the equator and is 496km (308 miles) from Male'. There is no airport and, until 2003, access was by beach landing in rough seas, which kept the people isolated and made it hard to export the island's agricultural produce. A constant swell around the island meant that fishing could only be done on the calmest days.

A harbour of 20,0000 sq m (215,000 sq ft) took three years to dredge and build, with sea walls 5m (16½ft) in height sustained by sheet piling and granite blocks imported from India. With a depth of 2.5m (8ft) the harbour can accommodate cargo vessels as well as passenger *dhoni*s and launches. It is a four-hour journey by *dhoni* (one hour by speedboat) from the airport at Gan in the next atoll.

To give access to the harbour, a surfaced ring road was constructed around the island and a land-use plan introduced to preserve the wetlands for recreation, and to set up an industrial zone, commercial areas and housing schemes. Cars and motorbikes were imported and the island is rapidly entering the modern world, and already has cyber cafés and mobile phones.

The island is mainly agricultural, producing grains, yams, mangoes, oranges, bananas and vegetables for sale in Male'. There are two freshwater lakes and much of the island is wooded, making it a lush and pretty place in its so far undeveloped interior. The population is about 9,000.

As one of the oldest inhabited islands in the Maldives, Foammulah has an impressive history. H.C.P. Bell in 1922 and Thor Heyerdahl 60 years later investigated Buddhist ruins, and there are ancient mosques, including the Kedeyre Mosque surrounded by beautifully carved tombstones. The

---

Ibn Battuta

Ibn Battuta (1304–77) was an indefatigable 14th-century traveller who managed to visit over 40 countries during a 24-year period after setting out from his native Tangier. As the first tourist, he visited the Maldives (known to him as Dhibat Almahal) and stayed for 18 months (1343–4) on his first visit. Having served as a judge in India, he was appointed chief judge and tried to impose his strict standards of moral behaviour on the islanders. He records with disappointment in his notes: 'I essayed to make the women dress themselves (cover their breasts), but in this I did not succeed.'

He also observed that 'all the food made from the coconut, and the fish eaten at the same time, effect an extraordinary and unequalled vigour on manhood.'

He describes the impressive hospitality of the islanders, adding that: 'Any of the newcomers who wishes to marry is at liberty to do so. When the time comes for his departure, he repudiates his wife, for the people of the Maldives do not leave their country.'

Ibn Battuta seems to have taken advantage of that hospitality since he claims to have married and divorced several women. Of his visit to Foammulah (Fua Mulaku), he wrote: 'I took with me one of my four wives… I remained at Muluk seventy days and married two wives there.'

Muslim traveller Ibn Battuta lived on the island in 1344 and wrote about his adventures there.

Addu Atoll

Accommodation for visitors on Foammulah is planned, but at present visitors stay on the southernmost atoll of the Maldives, **Seenu**, more popularly known as **Addu Atoll**. It is the second most populated atoll after Male' Atoll, with six inhabited islands set in a crescent with all the islands on its rim.

The population of more than 17,000 people live mostly on four islands linked by a new causeway, which

Feydhoo local

terminates in **Hithadhoo**, the capital. Hithadhoo is a developing town of about 10,000 inhabitants. It has a hospital, the Southern Secondary School, a bustling fish and cargo harbour, and streets of stores and teashops. The causeway was completed in 2003 to connect inhabited islands from the airport at Gan in the south to Hithadhoo at the northern tip of the crescent. It supports a broad highway, 12km (7½ miles) long, with a tarmac surface. With the sea on the northern side for its entire length, the broad highway matches the corniches of the Mediterranean in splendour and views. Where possible, trees have been left growing and coconut palms have been retained as a road divider. Raised pedestrian crossings and clear signposting have been created at strategic points, and new buildings and cafés have sprung up to cater for the needs of passing motorists.

At present there is only one hotel available for tourists, **Equator Village**, which was was built on the site of the former Royal Air Force base on **Gan**. Equator Village offers an experience unique outside Male': the chance to meet and mingle with Maldivians without having to make a special excursion. Bicycles or taxis can be hired for a visit by the new highway to Hithadhoo and to drop in at the village communities on the way. Technically, Gan is an uninhabited island. However, the causeway has made it part of the long southern coastal strip.

Historically, the people of Addu regarded themselves as being independent from the northern atolls and there used to be direct trading by sea with neighbouring Ceylon and India. Gan's ancient history was unearthed by H.C.P. Bell in 1922

RAF Memorial at Gan

when he investigated several ruins with Buddhist connections. One mosque dates to the 17th century. On the island of **Meedhoo** at the northeastern tip of the crescent there is an ancient cemetery known as Koaganu. **Hithadhoo** was known for its blacksmiths and jewellers, as well as for fishing.

On the causeway between Gan and neighbouring Feydhoo

Gan came to prominence when the British military landed in 1941 on its neighbouring island of **Viligili**. A Royal Air Force base with a long runway was set up on Gan, and there is a war memorial with the names of those who served and died there during World War II. Two big guns mounted by the memorial in 1972 formed part of the defences of the atoll. The British left at the end of the war but returned in 1956 to run the base as a staging post for military aircraft until leaving controversially in 1976. By then, British manners, discipline, and English as a language, had moulded the population. This is still apparent today, with many northern resorts hiring staff from Addu because of their British-influenced background.

For years Gan has seemed poised for development even if, because it is officially uninhabited, it seems rather quiet and somewhat regimented. In anticipation of tourism spreading to the atoll, the airstrip has been developed and upgraded and is capable of coping with long-haul jets. Viligili is now being developed as several resorts (expected to open in 2008), and other resorts are planned or being built in the atoll, including the intriguingly named island of **Herethere** (pronounced 'hairy-terryh', not 'here-there').

WHAT TO DO

Many resorts happily promote themselves as the place 'to do nothing' and Doing Nothing used to be the reason for holidaying in the Maldives. If you're inclined to be more active, 'what to do' will require a little initiative and some expense, because of the cost of getting away from the resort.

EXCURSIONS AND CHARTERS

If you want to have a day out, every resort organises excursions to the capital (if close enough), to a neighbouring village, to a deserted island for a picnic lunch, and even for a quick familiarisation visit to nearby resorts (if only to prove how much better than its neighbours is the resort you're staying on). However, there is no regular ferry service linking one island with another, so if you want to travel around, then you'll have to charter a boat, either from the resort or in Male'.

Chartering a *Dhoni*

With a fairly slow speed of about 13km/h (8mph), and bench seats and no facilities, a *dhoni* is convenient only for short distances, unless you charter a luxury one *(see Dhoni Mighili, page 78)*. *Dhonis* are used by resorts for diving and for village island excursions, so chartering one from a resort depends on availability.

In Male' there are plenty of *dhoni*s for hire and the place to go is Jetty No. 9, opposite the Nasandhura Palace Hotel, where *dhonis* running the service to the airport tie up. The skipper's willingness will depend on how brisk is the airport ferry business, his mood, what you are prepared to pay and whether he knows the route. The rate starts at US$25 per hour.

Travel in style with a speedboat

It is advisable to ask a local tour operator to handle the chartering negotiations as they will make sure the *dhoni* skipper understands your requirements and will even send someone along as guide and interpreter. A brief island-hopping trip could be arranged from Male', and *dhonis* can also be hired for the trip to the airport *(see pages 107–8).*

Chartering a Speedboat

If a *dhoni* is a taxi, a speedboat in the Maldives is the equivalent of a chauffeur-driven limousine, and costs proportionately more. For convenience, comfort and style, a speedboat is ideal for a quick visit to a resort, perhaps for dinner. While resorts are happy to arrange speedboat hire for their guests, in Male' this is best done through a tour operator. A company with its own fleet of speedboats for independent chartering is Inner Maldives Holidays, tel: 332 6309, <*www.innermaldives.com*>.

Speedboats generally have two 200hp engines and a captain and crew of two, plus satellite navigation aid and adequate life-saving equipment, as well as radio and mobile telephone communication. The chartering cost will be based on a point-to-point journey or a time charge plus fuel; expect the rate to start at US$100 per hour.

Chartering a Safari Boat

The best way to see the Maldives is to charter a 'liveaboard' vessel, known as a safari boat. This will have cabins for two with bunks, or a large common cabin with pairs of bunks separated by curtains. Toilets are seawater flushed, but there will be a freshwater shower. Meals are taken on deck or in the saloon.

There will be a captain and at least two crew members, together with a cook and a dive crew (with diving equipment carried on a separate *dhoni*), since most people charter a safari boat for diving expeditions rather than solely to cruise around the atolls. The boat's operators will put together a group of individuals to fill the boat, or it can be chartered in its entirety by a group of friends. Passenger capacity ranges from six to 30 and the cost includes the government tax payable per guest per night and all meals, with drinks and diving extra.

> **Diving from resorts is restricted to sites within a one- or two-hour radius by *dhoni*. Diving safari boats cover wider areas with a greater variety of sites.**

Safari boats usually operate on a regular, pre-arranged schedule because the skipper knows the best dive sites and which picnic and village islands can be visited without hassle. The boats anchor at night, sometimes near an amenable resort, allowing passengers to go ashore for a meal or drink.

Two safari boat operators are Inner Maldives Holidays, tel: 332 6309, <*www.innermaldives.com*> and Voyages Maldives,

Dhoni Mighili vessel

tel: 3323617, <*www.voyages maldives.com*>. A full list of operators is available from the Maldives Tourism Promotion Board, tel: 332 3228, <*www.visitmaldives.com*>.

Cruise by Luxury *Dhoni*

The resort known as **Dhoni Mighili** has six luxury, private *dhonis*. Each one has sails as well as an engine and a sun deck with plump cushions for relaxing, a huge air-conditioned cabin with a king-sized bed, an LCD screen and DVD player, and attached bathroom with hot-water shower. The galley is fully equipped for meals and drinks service.

Each has a young, *feyli-* (sarong-) clad Maldivian captain with a crew of two, plus personal valet *(thakaru)* in constant attendance. The *dhonis* can be used to transfer guests from the airport for a leisurely five-hour cruise to the resort, for diving and snorkelling, for sunset fishing cruises, or simply to sail through the islands. At night the *dhonis* tie up alongside the jetty of the resort island (Dhoni Mighili, tel: 666 0751, <*www.dhonimighili.com*>).

Cruise the Atolls

With two alternating weekly itineraries around the atolls, the Maldivian cruise ship *Atoll Explorer* combines the safari experience with smooth sailing and good service. There is a diving instructor and a diving station on board and a diving *dhoni* follows the ship.

Atoll Explorer, converted from an oil rig supply ship, has become very popular since she began cruising in the Maldives in 1997 (<*www.atollexplorer.com*>). Her 20 cabins (eight with private balconies) are compact with double or twin beds, clothes cabinet, lots of hooks and mirrors, individually controlled air conditioning, and en-suite bathroom with hot-water shower.

There are fore and aft sun decks (two Jacuzzis aft) linked by an open-sided deck converted with transparent screens into a light and airy restaurant. On the lower deck is an air conditioned bar and smoking lounge. Passengers are usually a jolly mix of young and old, divers and non-divers, so a house-party atmosphere soon develops.

Whale Submarine

The ship cruises to a new island during breakfast for guests to spend the day on a beach or swimming, diving or exploring. Lunch is served on board or at a beach picnic, with another island visit in the afternoon. The ship anchors in the calm waters of a deserted island at night, and each day ends with cocktails and a buffet dinner. On the last night the ship moors close to the airport and a band comes aboard for a farewell party.

Catch a Submarine

Whale Submarine is an underwater dive popular with children and older visi-

Maldivian Air Taxi

tors who might not want to try diving. This incredible experience takes place eight times a day, at scheduled diving times, from Male'. There is a booking office in Male' and another at the airport; bookings could also be made through the resort to combine with a Male' excursion.

The submarine, which holds 50 passengers and has a crew of three, dives first to 25m (80ft) to gaze at a colourful display of corals and fish. Descending another 15m (50ft) to a submerged reef, the submarine is surrounded by schools of blue or yellow striped snappers, lionfish and yellow box fish. Turtles, manta rays and occasionally sharks can also be seen.

A dive costs from US$75 per person and there are discounts for families, children and groups (Whale Submarine, tel: 333 3939, <*www.submarinemaldives.com.mv*>).

Seaplanes

Seaplanes make special photo flights and daytime visits to picnic islands. These flights can be booked through the resorts, and seaplanes can also be chartered by the hour. The companies are Maldivian Air Taxi, the world's largest seaplane operator, with 21 Twin Otters (tel: 331 5201, <*www.mataxi.com*>), and Trans Maldivian Airlines (tel: 332 5708, <*www.transmaldivian.com*>).

Village Island Visit

A visit to a village island as an excursion by *dhoni* is available from every resort, except Equator Village on Gan where guests can ride a bicycle or take a taxi to see village life *(see page 72)*. The excursion may also include a visit to a real desert – and deserted – island for a picnic lunch.

The first impression of an inhabited village island is of emptiness. There are houses and sandy streets, but where are the people? A typical day on a village island begins with the dawn prayer between 4.30am and 6am, then the fishermen get ready for the day, collecting baitfish stored in cages offshore, and set out to sea before sunrise. In the outside kitchens of the houses, women prepare breakfast, then they sweep the yards and roads and get the children ready for school.

Weavers, carpenters, craftsmen, toddy tappers and staff at the offices and shops on the island commence their work. Many of the island men will be away working on contract, either in hotels or on construction sites or factories, while teenage children will be studying at the atoll's education

A peaceful village lane

centre or in Male'. The women stay inside their houses or in the low-walled compound that forms the yard, engaged in cottage crafts like weaving mats from dried leaves and making rope from the fibre of coconut husks, or cooking. The younger children will be in school, and tourists are usually shown the school as well as the island hospital or clinic and the island chief's office.

It is interesting to visit the village shop to see the essentials on sale, but it may be closed if the owner is doing something else, or simply relaxing in a wayside *joli*, a village bucket-seat made from webbing hooked around a metal frame.

The older houses are made of coral, while newer ones use cement. The bathrooms are open air, with water drawn up by bucket from the compound's well. In villages where tourists are frequent there will be a shop or two selling souvenirs and soft drinks.

The silence of village islands is compounded by the lack of interest the inhabitants show in visitors. This is because of a natural reserve rather than a lack of friendliness. On some village islands, stalls selling souvenirs are set up especially, and are dismantled when the tourists leave. In the late afternoon, the fishing boats return and villagers and children gather at the beach to see the day's catch. The sun sets and the villagers prepare for evening prayers, before going to bed early.

SHOPPING

Every resort has at least one shop carrying basic toiletry essentials and suncreams; some have shops with souvenirs and a few books and there may be a jeweller. There are duty-free shops at the airport on departure where even alcohol can be bought. Also at the airport are a jeweller, a large perfume store, electronics and photographic counters, some clothes shops, a confectionary outlet and a book shop with a good selection of books about the Maldives.

Male' has watch and electronics showrooms, with almost duty-free prices, and a supermarket *(see page 30)*. The main shopping street for souvenirs is Chandhanee Magu, easily reached from the waterfront. Freelance guides who offer their services at the landing jetty will eventually steer visitors to those shops.

Apart from lacquer work and locally painted T-shirts, there are few other souvenirs actually made in the Maldives. Goods like masks, painted wooden fish, and shells, are imported. The local market has packets of island-made sweetmeats and nuts, and tuna-fish products can also be bought there. The sale of items of black coral, turtle, or large shells is banned.

The main shops in Male' open around 9am or 10am and will stay open, with 15-minute breaks at prayer times, until 11pm, every day except Friday when they open only in the afternoon.

The traditional hand-woven mat, the *kunaa (see following page)*

Maldivian Crafts

Maldivians were self-sufficient and skilled at craftwork until the demand for local, handmade items was killed by imported, machine-made products, a trend that even tourism cannot reverse in spite of the market for Maldivian-crafted souvenirs. They built mosques with coral stone and wood using basic tools and decorated them with elaborate, artistic carvings. They wove rush mats, coconut-leaf sails and used locally grown cotton to make hard-wearing fabrics.

The traditional hand-woven mat, *kunaa*, using Cyperacea rush *(hai)* dyed in black, brown and cinnamon gold, is produced by women on Gadhdhoo Island in Huvadhu Atoll. *Saanthi*, a type of mat used for sleeping, is woven from screwpine leaves, mostly by women in the northern atolls. *Roanu* – coir rope plaited from the dried fibre extracted from the husks of coconuts – is fashioned into webbing for the local bucket seat *(joli)*, for doormats and for mooring *dhonis*.

Rukufathi weaving is traditionally done by men, with the island of Bilehfahi in Shaviyani Atoll being famous for its production of kitchen-ware and containers from the long narrow strips cut from the stem of palm fronds. Coconut leaves are used by island craftsmen for fan products like boxes, including a triangular container known as *gonu*. *Bonthi fan* refers to young coconut leaves crafted into images and toys. The spine of the coconut leaf *(iloshi)* is turned into items such as the *mukabba* food cover traditionally crafted by men.

The weaving of gold and silver lace known as *kasabu* to decorate the neckline of a dress (the *kasabu libaas*) is done by women in the southern atolls of Addu and Huvadhu. They also produce *kinari* lace on a handloom from gold or silver thread.

Feyrankuran garments handwoven in colourful cottons on looms made of wood, bamboo and coir rope to traditional designs include *libaas* (a woman's dress), *mundu* (a man's sarong) and *rumaa* (scarf). The *feyli* black sarong with two white stripes and embroidered ends is woven on a similar handloom and is highly prized because of its uniqueness.

ACTIVE PURSUITS

Walking

Walking throughout Male' is pleasant and, because of the reserved nature of most Maldivians, foreigners are unlikely to be accosted by strangers. Maldivians like to stroll the streets of the capital after nightfall, and shops and street stalls are busier then. Around the Southern Harbour and the artificial beach area, young people promenade or sit at one of the many open-air cafés.

The resorts in Maldives are horizontal, rather than high-rise, so guests have to walk a lot, especially where

Beach volleyball

the jetty stretches out to deep water or if there are long jetties to reach overwater accommodation. Some resorts, like Soneva Fushi, Kuramathi and Island Hideaway are large with walking trails through the dense vegetation. Others are so small it takes only 10 minutes to walk around the entire island.

Sport

Football is popular on every island and as a spectator sport in Male', where various local league matches and regional games are played in the National Stadium. Other competitions held in Male' include volleyball and basketball, as well as cricket and tennis. On a resort, the staff often compete in beach **volleyball** games and guests are invited to join in.

Spas

Every resort worth its salt has added a spa facility in recent years as the demand has spread for something extra to do while on a beach island. The most famous is the underwater spa at Huva-fenfushi. New resorts have added spas over water, on a neighbouring island, in beach pavilions for two, in the jungle and in guests' rooms by appointment. Many of the therapists are from Thailand and the prices reflect the up-market nature of the treatments. There are also some spas in Male', but they lack the glamour of those in the resorts.

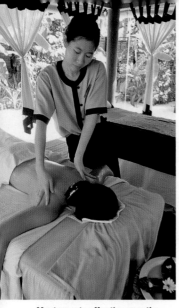

Most resorts offer therapeutic treatments

Diving

The Maldives is home to tens of thousands of reefs, a thousand recorded species of fish, over 200 species of coral, and hundreds of species of other marine life.

Only a small percentage of reefs have been dived. Because of the currents and elements that shape and mould the reefs, each dive site has unique characteristics in form, flora and fauna. The dive-centre staff at every resort know the best areas for beginners or experts to dive. At resorts like Baros that have a house reef close to the shore, guests can snorkel and dive without having to go on a boat trip to find good dive spots. This saves money and is the best option for beginners.

An estimated 40 percent of visitors go to the Maldives specifically to dive, while many others try it as something to do during their holiday. Diving is done year-round, with the water and skies usually clearer from January to April. In October and November there is more plankton, which attracts bigger fish, but the sea is less clear. Every resort has a diving centre, usually operated by an expatriate dive master. Instructors are fully qualified with up-to-date certification from one of the established institutions such as the Professional Association of Diving Instructors (PADI). All diving centres and schools are licensed by the government and are equipped with full safety facilities. There are two decompression chambers, one on Bandos and the other on Kuramathi. Divers are not permitted to go deeper than 30m (100ft).

Accessible Reefs

Experts can dive the six major underwater sites within easy reach of Male'. Located north of Soneva Gili resort, H P Reef is 100m long, with outcrops of coral, caves and crevices. Okobe (Barracuda) Thila, close to Bandos, consists of three reefs with an amazing variety of marine life. Manta Point, appropriately named for the mantas to be seen there, is part of the outside reef of Paradise Island.

Near Full Moon resort are the Furana North and Furana Thila, which have caves and sharks. Banana Reef, between Full Moon and Kurumba, offers fantastic underwater scenery as well as colourful fish. *Maldive Victory* is a ship that sunk south of the airport and offers a fascinating wreck dive. A buoy fixed to the ship's mast marks the spot.

Dive masters at new resorts in the northern and southern atolls are identifying reefs not previously explored and these might be of interest to divers who already know Male' Atoll's reefs. Diving from resorts is restricted to sites within a one- or two-hour radius by *dhoni*; safari boats *(see page 77)* cover wider areas with a greater variety of sites.

Diving is never done without supervision, and the instructors know the best dive sites in their atoll within easy reach by diving *dhoni*. Beginners are welcome and are given a supervised sample dive and a course lasting four to six days. The coveted Open Water Diver Certificate, which can be used as a licence to dive anywhere in the world, takes about nine days, allowing for theory as well as diving. The cost is from US$500, plus any equipment and boat-hire charges.

There are 25 protected marine dive sites in the atolls. At these locations, anchoring, fishing and destructive activities are prohibited.

Snorkelling

The beautifully clear water of a resort's lagoon soon entices even the complete novice to try snorkelling. Instruction is available at resort dive centres on how to snorkel. The

Colours of the reef

equipment of mask and flippers can be hired or bought on the resort, or in Male'. Life jackets are advisable and a T-shirt will stop your back getting sunburnt.

A number of resorts organise expeditions by *dhoni* for supervised snorkelling beyond the reefs. Spear fishing and harpooning fish are prohibited, as is removing coral, dead or alive, or any sea creature.

> A diving school in Male' uses chartered *dhonis* to take divers to a selection of 25 dive sites in North and South Male' atolls. Offering various PADI all-inclusive courses, the school is able to charge less than the resorts because its overheads are smaller. Contact Sea Explorers Associates (tel: 331 6172, <*www. seamaldives.com.mv*>).

Fishing

Fishing by net or rod and line in the lagoons is prohibited, so the resorts arrange fishing expeditions beyond the reefs. Popular, especially with those new to fishing, is **night fishing**. This involves setting out in a *dhoni* at nightfall to an area where the skipper judges fish are to be found. Each guest is given a simple line and

hook, which is baited by the boat crew, and shown how to dangle it over the side of the boat.

Patient waiting is invariably rewarded with a tug on the line at which a crew member helps the guest pull in the line and land the fish. The highlight of a night fishing session is having the catch barbecued on the beach afterwards.

Maldivian fishermen don't go out far

Despite their affinity with the sea, Maldivians generally do not fish far from their island as they prefer to return home at night. They fish with rod and line for tuna, scattering live bait or sprinkling water on the sea's surface and hooking in fish with deceptive ease.

Deep-sea fishing using boats specially constructed for big-game fishing, with equipment provided, has been introduced at some resorts, notably Full Moon. Costs range from US$500 for a morning. There is no particular season for game fishing for sailfish, blue and black marlin, yellow-fin and dogfish tuna, barracuda, wahoo, jack fish, sharks and dorado. Sailfish and blue marlin are tagged and released and all fish caught are the property of the boat.

Surfing
Surfing is the fastest-growing water sport in the Maldives, perhaps spurred on by waves that pound the southeastern

corner of Male', which enable local youths to learn at **Surfing Point** without having to go to a resort. There is good surf in North Male' Atoll between February and October, especially during the Southwest Monsoon from April onwards. Waves are about 2m (6½ft) high.

Kanu Huraa (formerly the resort of Tari Village then Dhonveli) and **Hudhuranfushi** (formerly known as Lohifushi), on the east side of North Male' Atoll, are famous for surfing. There are seven or eight surfing breaks within 15 minutes' *dhoni* ride from Hudhuranfushi, while surfing is possible within a five- to 10-minute paddle from the Hudhuranfushi shore. Surfing breaks there include Ninja, Lohi's, Pasta, Sultan, Cokes, Honkies, Chickens and Himafushi.

The large island of **Himafushi** is renowned for waves known as 'Jailbreak', while the industrial island of **Thulusdhoo** is known for good surf between April and October. The best 'lefthander' in the atoll is near **Kuda Villingili**. Waves in the channel between the southern atolls of Laamu and Gaaf Alif/Gauf Dhaal (**Huvadhu**) create top-class surfing when the northeast Monsoon blows, from December to March.

Other resorts where surfers are catered for are **Full Moon** and **Paradise**. Surf areas and the nearest islands are: Sultan at Kanu Huraa, Monkey at Full Moon, Tiger at Thulusdhoo, Kamana at Than'burudhoo, Nickys at Kanifinolhu, Arifs at Hudhuranfushi, Shyams at Kuda Villingili, and Jumbo at Paradise. A specialist in organising surfing holidays is Sun Travels & Tours (tel: 332 5977, <*www. sunholidays.com*>).

Surfer from Male'

Other Water Sports

All resorts offer watersports as an extra for their guests, although some have more facilities (such as jet-skiing and banana-boat riding) than others. Most resorts have **windsurfing** with introductory courses and boards available for renting. A watchman, with a rescue boat available, is required to be on the resort beach to see windsurfers don't go beyond his range of vision. Windsurfing is not allowed at night.

Local *dhoni* and catamaran **sailing** can be arranged at some resorts, as can **parasailing**, **waterskiing** and **canoeing**.

ENTERTAINMENT

Entertainment, whether in Male' or on a resort, is limited. Larger resorts have occasional disco evenings, resident bands or a modern music band visiting from Male'. A cultural evening would feature the traditional dance of the islands, called Bodu Beru.

Folk Music

With influences from the people of African, Arabian and Asian countries who settled in the islands, the folk music of the Maldives has evolved into a distinctive form expressing the islanders' lifestyle. Some of the traditional music and dances are kept alive by schoolchildren performing them on national occasions, while the most popular, Bodu Beru, is danced by village troupes for their own enjoyment or for resort displays.

Bodu Beru is similar to the songs and dances found in East Africa and commonly known as Baburu Lava ('Negroid song'). This is a group dance with about 15 participants (usually only men), featuring at least three drummers and a lead singer. They are accompanied by a small bell and an *onugandu*, a small piece of bamboo scraped to produce a rasping sound. The songs are a mixture of local, African and invented words and tell of heroism, romance and satire.

A performance of Bodu Beru

They begin slowly, building to a crescendo and a trance-like state among dancers. In resorts guests are urged to join in.

A performance of Thaara involves 22 men seated in two parallel lines facing each other, playing tambourines (*thaara* in Dhivehi). The players wear white sarongs and shirts with a green scarf around their necks. The music has an Arabic influence. The songs sung in Gaa Odi Lava also have Arabic roots and are performed to celebrate the completion of a task.

There are several dances involving an intricate interplay of sticks or batons. One example is the Dhandi Jehun, an hour-long energetic dance for 30 people. Bolimalaafath Neshun is a graceful dance performed by women and derived from the ceremonial presentation of gifts to the sultan. Maafathi Neshun is a festival dance for women accompanied by three drummers.

A version of the Indian pot dance, with dancers carrying water pots, is called Bandiyaa Jehun. The dancers, all women, beat on the pots with metal rings to mark time to drum accompaniment. A rarely seen dance – it survives on the island of Kulhudhuffushi in south Thiladhunmathi (Haa Dhaal) – is the mysterious Kadhaa Maali. The *kadhaa*, a copper plate beaten with a copper rod, and drums set the beat for 30 men dressed in ghoulish costumes, occasionally joined by solo dancers, in a ritualistic night performance to ward off evil.

CHILDREN'S MALDIVES

While some resorts have special clubs and carers for the children of guests, others leave children to their own devices. Since the resorts are without traffic, strangers and dangerous animals, resorts are ideal for children on holiday. Maldivians like kids and enjoy interacting with the children of foreign guests. However, some resorts, to preserve the tranquillity expected by their high-paying clientele, will not accept children under the age of 16.

Playground at the Island Hideaway resort

Festivals

Moveable festivals and holidays

Many of the nation's holidays are based on the Muslim lunar calendar and take place at a different time every year, according to the Gregorian calendar. The festival of *Ramazan* (or Ramadan), the ninth month of the Muslim year, is the most important of the nation's festivals and holidays. During this time, fasting for 30 days from sunrise to sunset is obligatory for all Maldivians. Although Male' restaurants are closed during the day, facilities on the resort islands remain open and guests would hardly be aware of the 30-day fast. The end of Ramazan is marked by the three-day holiday of *Eid al-Fitr*.

Other holidays that fall on different dates each year are:

Martyr's Day, recalling the death of Sultan Ali VI in 1558.
Hajj Day.
Eid Al-Adha, the four-day festival of sacrifice.
Islamic New Year's Day.
National Day (a two-day holiday), commemorating the ousting of the Portuguese in 1573.
Birthday of the Prophet Mohammed.
The day the Maldives embraced Islam.
Huravee Day, celebrating the victory over Indian occupation in 1752.

Fixed holidays

1 January *New Year's Day*.
26 and 27 July *Independence Days*. Commemorates the end of the British protection period.
3 November *Victory Day*. Celebrates victory over the Tamil mercenary invaders in 1988.
11 and 12 November *Republic Days*. Celebrates the founding of the Second Republic in 1968.
10 December *Fishermen's Day*. Celebrates the role of the fisherman in Maldivian society.

EATING OUT

The cuisine of the Maldives is, not surprisingly, fish-based, usually tuna, whether freshly caught, served as *valhoamas* (smoked) or as *hikimas* (boiled, smoked and sun-dried). Served with rice, this is the basic diet of Maldivians.

At pioneering resorts like Kurumba, Full Moon and Baros, there are several restaurants offering different cuisines, such as Chinese, Thai, Arabian, Indian, Japanese and Mediterranean. Newer resorts have followed that example but usually have only one restaurant with specialised cuisine. A resort's main restaurant, for guests staying on a full- or half-board plan with meals included in the cost of the room, generally features buffets. This enables the chefs to provide dishes that satisfy the appetites of the many nationalities staying at the resort. Some resorts emphasise lighter, healthier options on their buffets, with lashings of salads and fruits and lean meat.

Apart from fish, practically everything offered to guests in the resorts is imported. Vegetables and fruit are grown in the islands, but these are not of the consistent quality required by resorts. Some ingredients come from Sri Lanka and India, but most are sourced from suppliers in Europe, air-freighted via Singapore.

Vegetables at the market

For the visitor, this means top-quality ingredients prepared in familiar styles by international chefs, so even the most fastidious diner should feel satisfied. More adventurous visitors, who want to try some genuine

Preparing food at home

Maldivian dishes, could start with breakfast by asking in advance for a taste of what the staff are served.

Breakfast

The Maldivian breakfast is unique in the region and consists of *mas huni* and *roshi* with a side curry. The curry is not as fierce as a Sri Lankan or Indian curry, being creamier (through the use of coconut milk) with a spicy zest. *Mas* is fish and the breakfast dish consists of smoked, or local tinned, tuna mixed with grated coconut, sliced onions and chilli combined with lime juice.

Roshi is a bread made of flour, water, oil and salt formed into a dough rolled out into a thin round and cooked on a hot griddle. The traditional way to eat this breakfast is to tear off a piece of the *roshi* and use it to scoop up a ball of the fish mixture with the fingers of the right hand. This is washed down with plain tea.

Breakfast on the beach

The usual resort breakfast buffet, because guests want to start the day with something familiar, has dishes from different countries: fried egg and bacon for the British, cold meats and cheese for continental Europeans, and Oriental porridges, etc., for Asians.

Short Eats

To try genuine Maldivian dishes, including Maldivian vegetables like breadfruit or plantain chips, it is necessary to make a gastronomic expedition to Male'. The capital has over 50 teashops and cafés where true Maldivian dishes can be sampled for less than US$1 a meal.

It is usually difficult to see what a teashop is like inside as its windows are painted and doors are kept closed to keep out flies and dust. The best places are known by their reputation, so they don't find it necessary to advertise. Ask a Maldivian to recommend somewhere or, better still, invite a

Maldivian to join you for tea in one of them. That way you'll have someone to explain what all the delicious 'short eats' (little snacks) contain.

These short eats, called *hedhikaa*, are displayed on a counter under glass or plastic covers. It is best to point to the items that look interesting, rather than asking the names which are difficult to remember. Or request a selection of the café's specialities, which will be brought to the table together with a glass of water for each guest.

Many of the snacks are based on the samosa principle, made with pastry wrapped in different shapes around a filling, usually spicy and inevitably fish, and then deep fried. There are two kinds of fish ball, known as *gulha*, which both contain smoked fish. One has a soft pastry shell while the other has a crust so hard it needs strong teeth to crack it. Packets of hard *gulha* can be bought from the Local Market *(see page 28)* to take home as a tasty souvenir.

One short eat, looking like a square of dark sponge cake, goes by the name of *kulhi boakibaa*. It is firmer in texture than sponge since it is made with rice soaked in water overnight and mixed with smoked fish, onions, chilli, ginger and coconut. The mixture is kneaded and placed in a greased dish, baked, and cut into squares for serving. There is a sweet version, without the fish, served at tea time.

Short eats (little snacks) are popular as part of the tea-time tradition. Tea is taken at any time of the day, but most often at mid-morning and mid-afternoon.

Another sweet snack (the waiter asks whether sweet or savoury snacks are required) is called *honi fulhi*. It looks like a soft spring roll and is actually *roshi* filled with a paste of coconut, honey and water and shallow fried. Another surprise is a tiny edible parcel of crispy pastry containing an appetising blend of chopped cabbage, onions and hard-boiled egg (no fish). It is called *biskeemiya*.

The freshest fish dishes in Male' are to be found in the café above the Fish Market, a noisy place where fishermen relax after unloading their catch for sale in the market below. A favourite there is *mas roshi,* made from a dough of flour, water and coconut milk into the centre of which is placed a mixture of shredded fish, grated coconut, and the usual onions, chilli and lime juice. This dough is rolled into a ball around the filling, patted flat to form a round, and then flipped over a few times on a hot griddle until cooked. It's snapped up by eager customers at any time of day.

Maldivians are used to eating with the fingers of the right hand. A spoon and fork will be provided for tourists in a local café if requested.

Made in the Maldives...

Soft Drinks

As alcohol is not permitted in Male', cafés serve a variety of soft drinks, including non-alcoholic beer. Mineralised drinking water is bottled on the nearby island of Thulusdhoo where it is produced from desalinated sea water. Coca-Cola is made at the same plant, as well as other soft drinks, such as bitter lemon.

Maldivian fish curry

Maldivian Cuisine

Maldivians have their main meal at midday, with a lighter version of the same diet at night, or perhaps some short eats. A typical meal at a teashop or café is served in bowls for a customer to help himself according to his taste. He starts by ladling his plate full of boiled rice onto which he piles boiled breadfruit and boiled plantain. Next he adds a dash of fried fish and coconut chips, called *mas kurolhi*. Over this is poured a bowl of coconut milk and then a spoonful of a sticky tuna-fish paste called *rihaakuru*, to add a spicy seasoning.

A lighter dish is *garudhiya*, a clear soup with chunks of tuna and whole chillies floating in it, used as a sauce poured over boiled rice. Another, oddly palatable, dish is *mas bondibaiy*, a combination of sweet and sticky nutty rice pudding and chilli fried fish. Vegetables do not feature strongly in Maldivian cuisine, possibly through shortage in the past.

Chicken is becoming more easily available, particularly in the new generation of Male' cafés patronised by young professionals. One such dish is *kukulhu masama*, a smooth chicken curry. A Maldivian meal is always finished with a serving by tray of thinly sliced areca nut, betel leaves, cloves and lime paste. Combined and chewed together this acts as a digestive.

Teashops are gradually giving way to trendy-looking coffee bars catering to the Male' young set. At the coffee bars by the open-air theatre complex near the Hulhumale' ferry terminal, menus feature European fast-food items alongside desserts with local names, like *goma* and *thakuru* – glasses of ice cream mixed with sweet soda and flavoured syrup. Some cafés, such as **Seagull**, specialise in fresh fruit juices and locally made ice creams.

As well as the teashops and cafés, Male' has a broad range of restaurants offering a variety of fare. The ones

Areca nut and betel leaves – served at most cafés and teashops

attached to hotels have menus to cater for everyone, and the accent is on dishes with rice and grilled or fried items, including steak. Pork is not served in Male' but is available in the resorts. Restaurants in Male' are usually busy for lunch and quieter in the evenings. The Thai Wok is an exception as it is often packed at night and making a reservation in advance is necessary. Where there are menus (don't expect any in

Dinner place settings at a resort

the teashops), these are written in English, so ordering is easy, as long as the waiter, who might be from Bangladesh, not the Maldives, can understand you.

Some Menu Items

fruit	**meyvaa**	curry	**riha**
banana	**dhonkeyo**	fish curry	**mas riha**
mango	**anbu**	chicken	**kukulhu**
papaya	**falhoa**	meat	**eggamu-mas**
fish	**mas**	beef	**geri-mas**
reef fish	**faru mas**	mutton	**bakari-mas**
dried fish	**hikimas**	pork	**ooru-mas**
vegetables	**tharukaaree**	eggs	**bis**
potatoes	**aluvi**	water	**fen**
tea	**sai**	milk	**kiru**
short eats	**hedhikaa**	sugar	**hakuru**
rice	**baiy**		

HANDY TRAVEL TIPS

An A–Z Summary of Practical Information

A

ACCOMMODATION

With nearly 100 resorts, the style of accommodation ranges from the '*no shoes, no news*' basic tropical islands (which are not necessarily the cheapest) to high-end resorts where rooms are furnished like city apartments, some with a butler to boot. Since all resorts have glorious white-sand beaches, enticing, translucent lagoons, swaying coconut palms and an atmosphere of safety and seclusion, what you choose depends on whether you seek isolation or camaraderie, over-lagoon log cabins or four-unit room blocks.

Price is no guide to simplicity since one of the most expensive resorts, **Dhoni Mighili**, is also one of the smallest, with sand floors in its very informal reception/bar/restaurant, no cyber centre (although the manager's computer can be used in an emergency), and nothing organised. On the other hand, one of the lowest-priced resorts, the large **Kuredu**, offers lots to do, with five bars, five restaurants and golf.

Usually accommodation is provided as part of a holiday package, and resorts that cater exclusively for certain nationalities are only marketed in those countries. Thus Italian guests, who like a lot of organised activities, go for resorts where there are resident Italian-speaking activities organisers, which might not appeal to other nationalities.

Resorts provide a good standard of accommodation, with fans or air conditioning, bathrooms (sometimes set in an attached private garden open to the sky) with a shower that has fresh hot water. Not all have television and some don't have swimming pools, letting guests rely on the lagoon for a swim. Some have room service and an in-room kettle for making tea, and all have daily room cleaning done by a room boy, usually Maldivian.

Some islands have what are variously called water bungalows, water villas or water suites. If these are cement-block built, they do resemble bungalows, but most are made of wood and are more like up-market log cabins. They are built on cement pillars over the lagoon and are usually positioned so that their sun decks are not overlooked by neighbours. Many have steps down into the sea, and some feature a glass viewing panel set into the floor so that you can watch the fish swim past.

There are a few Maldivian companies that operate resorts, as well as the well-known international hotel chains, such as Hilton and Four Seasons. The Universal Enterprises company (*<www.universalresorts.com>*) is Maldivian-owned and runs and maintains its resorts to a high standard. Another local company, the Villa Group (*<www.villahotels.com>*), has several islands with a mass-market appeal.

On smaller, built-up islands the vegetation is not as lush as on larger islands that have only a few accommodation units. Paths are usually sand and all islands entail walking, either from the boat or water bungalow because the jetty extends a long way out into the lagoon, or from your room on one side of the island to the restaurant on the other. The more expensive resorts have golf buggies available. Few resorts have wheelchairs.

In Male' the hotel rooms are typically small and charmless. Accommodation is only available for foreigners in registered establishments and not at all on other inhabited islands, because there is a bed tax (US$8) payable by the establishment per guest per night. This tax is usually included in the resort room rate. There is no self-catering holiday accommodation and no camping.

AIRPORT

The entry point to the Maldives is Male' International Airport, which is situated on its own island (Hulhule). As you approach the airport by plane, it seems as if you are about to land on an aircraft carrier, because the runway extends into the sea. Passengers have to walk to or from the terminal, although buses are sometimes provided if it is raining.

There are toilets before the immigration counters, but no duty-free shops on arrival. Luggage trolleys are available in the baggage hall beyond the immigration desks. There is a bank and a counter with tourist information run by the Maldives Tourism Promotion Board at the exit from customs. Resort representatives with name boards meet arrivals there to steer them towards transfer boats, the seaplane check-in desks or one of the 60 counters manned by tour operators and hotel reps. There are no airport taxis, but a public ferry departs for Male' every 15 minutes.

A number of shops and facilities are located in the public departure concourse: toilets, a shower, a medical centre, a pharmacy, a post office, a florist, a book shop, cyber café, snack bar with a large sitting area, and an ice-cream parlour. All baggage is X-rayed at the entrance to the check-in hall. There are separate business and economy class check-in desks. Check-in commences three hours before a flight's departure.

The duty-free floor upstairs is popular with tourists who have had little chance to shop in their resorts. There is another snack bar adjoining it with seating space, a smoking room and a business-class lounge (tel: 333 5566). No alcohol is served at the airport, but it can be bought from the duty-free shop.

There is a security check by X-ray and a body search at the entrance to the departure gates, where there are toilets and another glass-walled room for smokers.

For flight information, tel: 332 2211. There is an airport hotel, **Hulhule Island Hotel** (tel: 333 0888, <www.hih.com.mv>), which is reached by shuttle bus from the arrivals concourse.

There is a regular ferry service by *dhoni* to the airport from Jetty No. 9 near the Nasandhura Palace Hotel in Male'. Passengers are dropped at the quay closest to the departure terminal. Ferries from the airport leave from the jetties where the resort boats pick up passengers. There is a ferry to and from Male' every 15 minutes during the day and a fare of MRf10 per person. *Dhonis* can also be chartered for the 10-minute crossing at MRf75 during the day, MRf100 after sunset and MRf150 after midnight.

People visiting the airport and who are not travelling anywhere should buy a permit from the security hut at the end of the boat arrival pier.

B

BICYCLE HIRE

Some resorts (like Equator Village) have bicycles for hire for a modest amount, while others (such as Island Hideaway) provide bicycles free of charge as a way for guests to get around a large island. There is no bicycle-hire service in Male'.

BUDGETING FOR YOUR TRIP

Even if you are staying at a resort that is all-inclusive, there are bound to be extras, such as laundry fees and tips for the room boy, so come prepared with cash (US currency) in small amounts. There is a head tax, currently US$8 per person per night and this is usually included in the room rate. Prices are given in US dollars, which is legal tender in the Maldives, and you will be billed in dollars; a 10 percent service charge will be added.

Getting There

Package holidays include flights either by scheduled or chartered airlines. Flying independently from Europe could cost around US$1,500 return. Some resorts add the transfer charge from/to the airport in Maldives, which could be an extra US$200 per person return, more if by seaplane.

Accommodation

There is accommodation available at resorts, even in high season if booked well in advance, at less than US$150 for two, full board. On the other hand, the price for a double at one of the up-market resorts could be around US$600, rising to beyond $1,000 for bed and breakfast.

Package holidays in 2007 with charter flights and accommodation for seven nights on a resort with overwater rooms, were being advertised in British newspapers from £845 to £1,245 per person, sharing a double room, all inclusive.

Meals and Drinks

Resorts offering only a bed-and-breakfast rate usually have at least a coffee shop for independent dining or charge a fee to cover meals in the main restaurant. Expect to pay US$35 per person for a set menu or buffet dinner, more if à la carte. Where breakfast and dinner is included in the room rate, there will be a coffee shop for snack lunches, perhaps about US$20. Beer is about US$5 a glass, cocktails around US$8, and wine from US$20 a bottle. Bottled mineral water is sometimes free in the bedrooms but could cost US$5 at the table.

Local Transport

There is no scheduled local transport. Buggies and bus rides (as on Kuramathi) are free on demand. Taxis in Male' cost MRfs15 (US$1.17). Transfers to and from a resort depend on whether you take a slow *dhoni* or a fast speedboat, and the distance. For independent trips, a *dhoni* could cost US$25 an hour, a speedboat from US$100 per hour.

Water Sports

The new, more expensive resorts generally charge more, on top of their room rates, for extras like water sports because of their higher infrastructural costs. A diving course could cost from US$500, a single dive around US$35; a snorkelling course from US$50, with equipment hire from US$10 per day. Windsurfing could cost about US$20 an hour, water skiing about US$5 a minute. For deep-sea fishing allow a minimum of US$500 for up to four people for a morning.

C

CAMPING

There are no campsites on the Maldives and camping is not encouraged. However, some resorts are willing to arrange for guests to stay on a neighbouring desert island for a day, or overnight in temporary accommodation.

CAR HIRE

Since the resorts have neither cars nor roads, there is no provision for self-drive hire cars, even in Male'.

CLIMATE

With its tropical climate, the Maldives experiences only minor variations in temperature throughout the year. The average maximum is 31°C (88°F), the average minimum 25.5°C (78°F). Humidity is around 80 percent and the average amount of sunshine every day is eight hours. However, it does rain, which is a blessing as it enables vegetation to flourish. Average rainfall in a year is less than 2,000mm (80in).

The period when the weather is at its best coincides with the northern hemisphere's winter, hence it is the peak holiday season. There are no cyclones, and severe storms are rare, climate and weather being governed by two monsoons.

	J	F	M	A	M	J	J	A	S	O	N	D
Max °C	29	29	30	31	31	30	29	29	29	29	29	29
Min °C	23	24	25	27	26	25	24	25	25	24	23	23
Max °F	84	84	86	88	88	86	84	84	84	84	84	84
Min °F	73	75	77	81	79	77	75	77	77	75	73	73

The northeast Monsoon season, which brings hot days and cooler nights and clear blue skies, is approximately from December to April, with tradition dating it specifically from 10 December to 7 April. The Southwest Monsoon, with winds from the opposite direction, is supposed to last from 8 April until 9 December. While it doesn't rain every day, and temperatures remain high, strong winds and heavy rainfall can occur at this time. Rain is usually spasmodic, coming late in the day after a sunny morning.

The sun is strong, even when shaded by clouds, and sunscreen of some kind should be worn.

CLOTHING

However much you feel like throwing off all your clothes in the heat and surrendering to the tropical sun, don't. Nudity is forbidden, except within one's own private accommodation – but not on deck on a safari boat even if privately chartered. Nude sunbathing on a beach could result in a fine of US$1,000. So as not to cause offence to local people, when visiting inhabited islands women should be covered from shoulders to knees, and men should avoid wearing brief shorts. Beach wear is best for resorts during the day, with smart-casual, stylish clothes for evening drinking, dining and visiting.

In the tropics cotton is the best as synthetic fibres attract the heat. T-shirts are fine and useful to keep off the sun while snorkelling. Loose-fitting garments in soft colours (not black) will help you keep cool. A hat helps protect from the sun's rays, while flip-flop slippers and sandals are easiest to remove to walk in the sand, or when visiting someone's house or a mosque.

It is unlikely you'll need a raincoat and, anyway, umbrellas are more practical in warm, tropical rain. To protect from fierce air conditioning in some restaurants, a light stole over bare shoulders is useful for women. A man would rarely need a jacket, or tie, and there is no occasion for formal evening wear.

Maldivians themselves dress fashionably and smartly. The veil, concealing the whole of the face except the eyes, is prohibited as it hides one's identity. Footwear that can be taken off easily is essential because shoes or sandals must be removed before entering a mosque and it is customary to do so when entering private homes (so as not to drag in a lot of sand).

CRIME AND SAFETY

Resort bedrooms have safes, or valuables can be locked in the hotel's secure safety deposit boxes against a receipt. Crime on resort islands is virtually unknown. If something disappears, it has probably been mislaid. If you intend claiming on your travel insurance for something missing, report it to the resort's management and obtain a signed copy of your report. All resorts have their own security service in operation, usually invisible, and strangers at a resort, perhaps on an island-hopping excursion, are discreetly monitored.

In Male' there are occasional household robberies and there is a drug problem, leading to social disturbances and crime.

For personal safety while diving or on a boat listen to your escort or guide. There are safety briefings given on all transfer boats as they leave the airport, and on all domestic flights.

CUSTOMS AND ENTRY REQUIREMENTS

For tourists from all countries, permission to stay for 30 days is stamped into the passport, together with a stamp saying 'Employment Prohibited'. Few tourists stay longer, but if an extension is needed, the local tour operator or resort will advise what to do. There is no need for a tourist to obtain a visa in advance.

Most tourists arrive with accommodation already arranged. If you cannot show evidence of booked accommodation, you will be asked to make a hotel reservation from the airport and supply immigration authorities with the address. All tourists are expected to have return air tickets. If not, you will have to buy one before being given permission to stay. Visitors are expected to have the equivalent of at least US$25 in cash or traveller's cheques for every day of their stay. You'll need that much anyway.

All incoming luggage is X-rayed and, if the customs officers are satisfied, there will be no further baggage check. Prohibited items include alcohol, pornography, pork, dogs, idols for worship, weapons, spear guns and illegal drugs. Any alcohol you have brought inadvertently will be retained in bond for collection on departure. There is a departure tax, currently US$12; this is usually included in the air ticket cost.

D

DRIVING

Driving, because roads are busy and short, is slow. Where the road is wide enough, vehicles drive on the left. There are traffic lights and light-controlled pedestrian crossings in Male'.

E

ELECTRICITY

Every resort supplies its own electricity by generator hidden as far away from the rooms as possible. The current is 240 volts AC at 50Hz, the same in Male' where electricity is supplied by the State Electric Company. Maintenance is good, although there can be breakdowns so a small torch could be useful for emergencies. Some hotel rooms have electric switches in inconvenient places and a torch could anyway be useful at night, as well as to light the path home after an evening in the bar.

Both three-pin square and round sockets are used, so an adapter may be necessary for charging mobile telephone batteries, etc. The more expensive resorts include hairdryers.

EMBASSIES, CONSULATES AND HIGH COMMISSIONS

The countries with high commissions in Male' are **Bangladesh** (tel: 331 5541), **India** (tel: 332 3015), **Pakistan** (tel: 332 3005) and **Sri Lanka** (tel: 332 2845). There are honorary consuls for a few countries, including the **UK** (c/o Dhiraagu, tel: 331 1218), **Germany** (c/o Universal Enterprises, tel: 333 2240) and **New Zealand** (tel: 332 2432).

Other embassies or high commissions are based in Colombo, Sri Lanka (dial 00 94 11 to access these numbers):

Australia: 3 Cambridge Place, Colombo 7, tel: 269 8767
Canada: 6 Gregory's Road, Colombo 7, tel: 522 6232
UK: 190 Galle Road, Colombo 3, tel: 243 7336
USA: 210 Galle Road, Colombo 3, tel: 244 8007

EMERGENCIES

On a resort any emergency should be reported immediately to reception. All resorts have fire-fighting procedures. Lifeguards are not generally posted by swimming pools and beaches, although water sports and dive staff are trained to handle emergencies. There are decompression chambers on Bandos in North Male' Atoll and Kuramathi in Ari Atoll. *Dhoni*s and speedboats are equipped with life vests and radios.

Some emergency phone numbers:

Police: **119**   Ambulance: **102**   Fire: **118**

F

FERRIES

Ferries run between the airport and Male' every 15 minutes during the day; the fare is MRf10. There are also regular ferries to the satellite residential islands of Villingili (from the Southern Harbour terminal; fare MRf3), and to Hulhumale' (from the terminal by the Nasandhura Palace Hotel; fare MRf5).

On Fridays there is a ferry service from Jetty No. 7 to Kuda Bandos at 8.30am; the fare is US$5 for foreigners. There are no ferries serving the resorts.

FLIGHTS

Scheduled flights to the four domestic airports from Male' International Airport are operated by Island Aviation Services Ltd (tel: 333 5566, <*www.island.com.mv*>), which uses 16-seater Dornier and 36-seater Dash-8 aircraft. Because foreigners cannot make a flight to another island without having made prior arrangements for accommodation, seat bookings are made by the resort being visited or by the agency representing the passenger.

The most popular flights for visitors are to the southernmost airport at **Gan** in Addu Atoll *(see page 72)* to stay at Equator Village, and to the northernmost one at **Hanimaadhoo** in Haa Dhaal Atoll, either for a day excursion to Utheem or to stay at Island Hideaway *(see page 57)*. Fares for foreigners are double those paid by locals.

Seaplane

The seaplanes are 16-seater Twin Otter aircraft, which have been specially converted with floats, instead of wheels, and they land only on the sea. At many resorts the landing area is marked by a buoy and the resort's *dhoni* transfers passengers to and from the plane. Other resorts have pontoons as an arrival and departure platform. Some, like the Hilton Resort in Ari Atoll, have a landing jetty and even a departure lounge.

The seaplanes are based at Male' International Airport, where there are landing jetties on the far side of the main runway. Sometimes seaplanes will moor at an island if guests are leaving in the early morning. Usually the cost of the seaplane transfer is included in the resort's room rate and the resorts arrange the transfer. Seats cannot be booked by individuals. However, if there is space available, it is sometimes possible to pay for a flight to a resort and back in the same plane, but passengers wouldn't have a chance to visit the resort because the plane takes off again after only 10 minutes.

G

GAY AND LESBIAN TRAVELLERS

There is no gay or lesbian culture apparent in the Maldives and no resort catering specifically for gay and lesbian visitors. Maldivians are discreet and expect visitors to conduct themselves in the same manner in public. Same-sex relations are illegal and offenders could face lengthy prison sentences and fines if convicted.

GETTING TO THE MALDIVES

The only regular scheduled airline with a non-stop service from Europe to Male' is Sri Lankan Airlines, with flights from London on weekends. Other flights with Sri Lankan Airlines involve a change of aircraft in Colombo. In the winter season, LTU operates to Male' from Munich and Austrian Airways from Vienna. Charter services are operated by Monarch, Condor and other airlines arranged through tour operators.

Emirates Airlines operates a daily scheduled flight from its hub at Dubai that connects with flights from Europe, as does Qatar Airways via Doha. Singapore Airlines has a daily flight from Singapore. Male' is also served by scheduled flights from India, Kuala Lumpur and Bangkok. There are daily flights from Colombo by Sri Lankan and Emirates airlines and it is possible to buy return tickets to Male' at Colombo airport (about US$300, depending on taxes and surcharges) to use as an add-on to a cheap flight from Europe to Colombo.

Only economy- and business-class seats are available, as there are no first-class seats on any aircraft serving Male'. From the

United States, a connection via Singapore, London or Dubai (from New York) would be the best option.

Small cruise ships (such as *Hebridean Spirit*) sometimes visit the Maldives and could be used as a pleasant way of getting there by sea. There are bunkering facilities at Island Hideaway Marina and Spa (<*www.island-hideaway.com*>) for those visiting by yacht.

GUIDES AND TOURS

All resorts arrange tours within their atoll, both island-hopping (to see a village island, a beach picnic island and another resort) and excursions to Male'. Maldivian Air Taxis (tel: 331 5201, <*www.mataxi. com*>) and Island Aviation Services Ltd (tel: 333 5566, <*www. island.com.mv*>) arrange photo flights and occasional tours to historic or picnic sites. An underwater tour from Male' by Whale Submarine (tel: 333 3939, <*www.submarinemaldives.com.mv*>) can be arranged.

A safari boat could be chartered for an ad-hoc tour or there are weekly scheduled tours of the atolls by the *Atoll Explorer* (tel: 333 2262, <*www.atollexplorer.com*>). Tours could be arranged through local tour operators, such as Inner Maldives Holidays (tel: 332 6309, <*www.innermaldives.com*>), Sea Explorers Association (tel: 331 6172, <*www.seamaldives.com*>), Crown Tours (tel: 332 9889, <*www.crowntoursmaldives.com*>) and Voyages Maldives (tel: 332 3617, <*www.voyagesmaldives.com.*)

There are no tour buses with guides operating in Male'. Freelance guides, with a good knowledge of the city and its history, are available at the landing quay.

H

HEALTH AND MEDICAL CARE

No vaccinations are required by visitors to the Maldives, unless they are flying from a yellow fever area. There is a Health Information Card attached to the Immigration Card that requests visitors to report to the Port Health Authority (tel: 332 3963) if they succumb to a fever. The idea is to keep Maldives free of malaria.

Medical care in Male' is good, with a private hospital (ADK, tel: 331 3553, <*www.adkenterprises.com*>) – which has doctors on hand for consultations without an appointment – as well as the state-run Indira Gandhi Memorial Hospital (tel: 333 5335, <*www.igmh.gov.mv*>. Male' has a lot of pharmacies for emergency medicines.

Each resort has a doctor on call, and the larger resorts have a resident doctor and nurse and a daily clinic. Tourists should have insurance to cover the cost of any medical treatment and evacuation from a resort by air if necessary.

Sensible precautions associated with holidaying in a hot climate will help prevent ill health. Avoid sunburn. Bottled mineral water should be drunk in preference to local tap water. To be secure, if you are not a frequent visitor to the tropics, a course of inoculations against diphtheria, tetanus, polio, typhoid and hepatitis A is sometimes recommended, and against cholera if there is an outbreak in the country from which you are flying, such as from India.

Mosquitoes and sand flies can be a nuisance, so a repellent might be useful. Bring sufficient supplies of your usual medicines in case replacements are not available locally.

HOLIDAYS

The following are holidays fixed according to the Gregorian calendar:

1 January	New Year's Day
26 and 27 July	Independence Days
3 November	Victory Day
11 and 12 November	Republic Days
10 December	Fishermen's Day

Friday is a holiday. There are also holidays, on different dates each year, to celebrate the Islamic festivals of *Hajj*, *Eid al-Adha*, New Year, National Day, the Prophet Mohammed's birthday, the day Maldives embraced Islam, Huravee Day, Martyr's Day, and the beginning and ending of *Ramazan (see page 95)*. While shops and restaurants are closed during these holidays, life in the resorts for guests seems no different from any other day. Christmas Day and New Year's Eve are not holidays, but the resorts arrange celebrations for guests to commemorate the occasions.

████████████████ █ ████████████████

ISLAND NAMES

Each atoll has two names, its traditional geographical one and its administrative code name derived from letters of the Dhivehi alphabet. The atolls, from north to south are:

North Thiladhunmathi	**Haa Alif**
South Thiladhunmathi	**Haa Dhaal**
North Miladhunmadulu	**Shaviyani**
South Miladhunmadulu	**Noonu**
North Maalhosmadulu	**Raa**
South Maalhosmadulu	**Baa**
Faadhippolhu	**Llaviyani**
Male'	**Kaaf**
Ari	**Alif**
Feldihu	**Vaavu**
Mulakatholu	**Meemu**
North Nilandhe	**Faafu**
South Milandhe	**Dhaal**
Kolhumadulu	**Thaa**
Hadhdhunmathi	**Laamu**
North Huvadhu	**Gaaf Alif**
South Huvadhu	**Gaaf Dhaal**
Fuvah Mulah	**Gnaviyani**
Addu	**Seenu**

L

LANGUAGE

The language of Maldivians is known as Dhivehi and is spoken only in the islands and in its Indian neighbour, the island of Minicoy lying to the north as one of the Laccadive islands. It belongs to the Indo-Aryan group with a link to Sanskrit. It is peppered with words from Arabic, Hindi, Sinhala, Urdu, Tamil, Parsi and English.

Dhivehi is spoken by all Maldivians, although there are differences in words and pronunciation according to region. Since 1960, English has been the medium of secondary education and is spoken throughout the country.

The language is written in Dhivehi script and printed from right to left. However, all menus and notices concerning foreigners are printed in English. While the visitor may try to learn a few words in Dhivehi, it is a complex language with different words to use according to the status of the person being addressed. Maldivians dealing with foreigners are quite at home with English.

A useful phrase is *Assalaam Alaikum*, a common greeting in Arabic among Muslims, meaning 'Peace be with you.' Here are some more phrases:

How are you?	**Haalu kiheneh?**	one	**ekeh**
		two	**dheyh**
Good.	**Raganlhu.**	three	**thineh**
I am going.	**Aharen dhanee.**	four	**hathareh**
		five	**faheh**
Where?	**Kobaa?**	six	**haeh**
When?	**Kon iraku?**	seven	**hatheh**
Thank you.	**Shukuriyyaa.**	eight	**asheh**
yes	**aan**	nine	**nuvaeh**
no	**noon**	ten	**dhihaeh**

M

MAPS

Gift shops in Male' (and the post office at the airport) stock a long (96-cm/38-in) laminated dark blue map (27cm/11in wide) that shows all the atolls, islands, resorts, diving points and surfing locations to scale. It's good enough for framing as a souvenir. The reverse shows Male' and Ari atolls in greater detail. A caption says: 'Not to be used for navigational purposes.'

For that an Admiralty Chart is the answer. These can be obtained in the United Kingdom from Marine Chart Services (<*www.marinechartservices.co.uk*>).

Atoll Editions of Australia have produced an *Atlas of the Maldives,* which can be bought in Male' and in resort gift shops.

There is a map of Male' in the free *Visitors' Guide* produced every year by the Maldives Tourism Promotion Board (<*www.visitmaldives.com*>).

MEDIA

There are three daily newspapers published in Male' – *Aafathis, Haveeru* and *Miadhu.* They carry a few pages in English. They are not available in the resorts, but some resorts print up Internet newspapers for their guests. The *Maldives News Bulletin* in English is issued weekly, often a few weeks' late, by the Maldives News Bureau of the Ministry of Information.

Television Maldives has an English news broadcast every day and relays some CNN programmes. Most resorts receive satellite TV programmes, and where there is no TV in the rooms, there is a TV lounge by reception.

Two books about the Maldives by Royston Ellis, the author of this guide, are available in Male'. These are *A Man for All Islands,* the biography of President Maumoon Abdul Gayoom, and *A Hero in Time*, a historical novel about Mohamed Thakurufaan.

MONEY

Currency. The United States dollar is legal tender and can be used for payment in resorts and in Male', although the change will probably be given in rufiyaa. The local currency is the Maldivian rufiyaa (MRf). Notes are available in 5, 10, 20, 50, 100 and 500 rufiyaa denominations.

Currency Exchange. There is a branch of the Bank of Maldives at the exit from the customs hall at Male' International Airport, where foreign currency can be exchanged into rufiyaa. The exchange rate is based on the fixed rate of Maldivian rufiyaa to the US dollar which, at press time, was last set in December 2004 at MRf12.75 for US$1.00. There are no restrictions on the import or export of currencies.

Credit Cards. The credit cards generally accepted by all resorts and by the main shops in Male' are MasterCard, Visa and American Express. These cards can also be used for obtaining cash at automatic teller machines in Male'.

Traveller's Cheques. Traveller's cheques are best used for changing into cash on arrival at the airport bank or for paying resort bills, since changing them into rufiyaa at banks in Male' can take time, and would require you to go to Male' to do it.

ATMs. Automatic teller machines (ATMs) have recently been introduced in Male', and one can be found outside the Bank of Maldives branch at the STO Trade Centre in Orchid Magu, as well as at the head offices of banks along the waterfront Bodu Thakurufaanu Magu. There are none on the resort islands.

Banks. There are five banks, with only the Bank of Maldives having branches in Male', Hulhumale', Villingili, at the airport, and at

Gan as well as in other main residential islands. Other banks, with offices in Male', are the Bank of Ceylon, Habib Bank, HSBC and the State Bank of India.

O

OPENING TIMES

Shops. Some convenience 'daily needs' small shops open from 6am or 7am, while in Male' the main shops open from 9am or 10am. All close at 11pm and have short breaks during the day at prayer times. On Fridays they open at 1.30pm, closing at 11pm. At resorts, the gift shop is usually open in the morning, late afternoon and in the evening.

Business and Offices. Government offices: Sunday to Thursday 7.30am–2.30pm, closed Friday and Saturday. Private offices: Sunday to Thursday 8am or 10am to 6pm or 8pm; closed Friday with some open on Saturday.

Post Offices. Sunday to Thursday 8am–6pm, Sat 10am–4pm, closed Friday.

Banks. Sunday to Thursday 8.30am–1.30pm, closed Friday and Sat.

Museum. Sunday to Thursday and Saturday 8am–6pm, closed Friday and holidays.

Restaurants. Teashops: 5am–1am; coffee shops: 9am–1am; most restaurants open for lunch, some close in the afternoon and reopen for dinner, and finally close at 11pm.

P

POLICE

On resorts, policing is done by private security firms, and any matters requiring police attention should be reported to the resort management. If a claim against insurance is likely, a signed report should be obtained. On inhabited islands, the island chief has the power to summon police if needed.

POST OFFICES

The main post office, called Atoll Post, is in Male' a few blocks east of the fish market. There is a post office shop in the public area of the airport. Inhabited islands have postal agencies. Mail posted in a resort will be hand delivered to the Atoll Post office for despatch. Incoming mail to resorts is delivered to the resort's Male' office or PO box for onward delivery by the resort's staff. The main international courier companies are represented in Male'.

PUBLIC TRANSPORT

There is a public bus service on Hulhumale' but none in Male' where taxis are used to get around.

Although there are over 600 taxis in the capital, they are not always easy to find, especially when it is raining. They are air conditioned, so passengers like riding in them even for a short journey just to keep cool. Taxis do not cruise the streets looking for hire, although empty ones can be waved down if not already booked.

The usual way to hire a taxi is to phone for one. The staff of any shop, restaurant or hotel will willingly telephone the nearest taxi centre and the taxi usually arrives within minutes. Taxis are conventional saloon cars, mostly Japanese, and the driver will be Maldivian, sometimes living in another island and in the capital for the day job.

While drivers know prominent landmarks and shops, they may not be familiar with the names of all the alleys and side streets, so it is advisable to know where a particular address is near. Taxis can be hired by the hour (at about six times the one-way drop fare), and for touring Male' at a negotiated price. The one-way fare to any destination is MRf15. Luggage is an extra MRfs5 per piece. Tipping is not customary but it won't be refused.

Some taxi services and their phone numbers: Dial Cab 332 3132, Dial Services 331 3130, Fine Taxi 332 1411, J R Taxi 332 1919, Kulee Dhuveli 332 2122, Loyal Taxi Service 332 5656, New Taxi Service 332 5757, Rasal Taxi Service 332 9292, Regal Taxi 332 1313.

Self-drive cars and motorbikes are not available for hire. While a bicycle is an ideal form of transport for getting around Male', there is no hiring centre for them. However, they can sometimes be borrowed from a guesthouse.

R

RELIGION

Every Maldivian is a Sunni Muslim. Religion is a vital part of the fabric of daily life and every inhabited island and resort has a mosque; Male' has over 20 mosques. Religious observance is strict, with prayers five times a day and fasting at *Ramazan*, even by Maldivians working in resorts. The president is the supreme authority entrusted with the protection of religion.

T

TELEPHONE

The main telephone service is provided by the Dhiraagu company, which offers fixed, mobile and Internet services covering all atolls. A mobile-phone service is also provided by Al Wataniya. There are prepaid card-operated public phones throughout Male' and in inhabited islands and in the staff areas of resorts. Most resorts have IDD facilities in guest rooms, or overseas calls can be made through reception.

The international IDD code for the Maldives is 960. All numbers have seven digits, with the first three numbers as the area code indicating the atoll. To call overseas from the Maldives, the international access code is 00.

Customer services **123**

Directory enquiries **110**

International telephone operator **190**

Mobile phones work in the resorts and on inhabited islands, but dip out of range during sea journeys between islands.

TIME ZONES

Officially the time in Maldives is GMT +5. However, some resorts set their own time, making a difference of one hour between resort time and Male' time. Maldives time is 30 minutes behind the time in neighbouring India and Sri Lanka. Because of their location so close to the equator, the islands experience little seasonal variation in daylight hours.

TIPPING

The custom of tipping has been introduced by visitors and, although the government does not encourage it and resort staff won't necessarily expect it, be prepared to reward special services. The staff who carry bags between jetty and room could be tipped US$1 per bag. There is a service charge (10 percent) added to bar drinks and meals. At the end of a holiday, some tour operators recommend about US$5 a day per guest to give individually to table waiters and room boys who have been especially helpful. In up-market resorts where the valet/butler is in constant attendance, allow US$10 or US$20 a day for him.

Taxi drivers and the staff serving in teashops do not expect tips.

TOILETS

There are some public toilets in Male', but visitors should use those attached to restaurants and hotels, such as the Nasandhura Palace Hotel. There are toilets on arrival and departure at Male' International Airport.

TOURIST INFORMATION

The Maldives Tourism Promotion Board (MTPB) has its main office on the fourth floor of the Aage Building in Bodu Thaku-rufaanu Magu, Male' 20094, tel: 332 3228, fax: 332 3229, email: *mtpb@visitmaldives.com,* website: *<www.visitmaldives.com>*. There is a counter at the arrivals exit of the airport. The Board issues a Visitors' Guide and a Directory of Hotels every year, as well as other promotional literature.

There is a representative of MTPB in the UK: McCluskey International Ltd, 4 Vencourt Place, London W6 9NU, tel: 020 8237 7979, <www.mccluskeyinternational.co.uk>.

W

WEBSITES AND INTERNET CAFÉS

Website service information is available from: <www.dhivehinet.net.mv>, <www.wataniya.mv> and <www.focus infocom.com.mv>.

Websites with information on the Maldives include:

<www.visitmaldives.com> the website of the Maldives Tourism Promotion Board.

<www.haveeru.com> the site of a daily newspaper with some local news in English.

<www.airports.com.mv> for information about the airport.

<www.maldivespost.com> for postal information.

<www.presidencymaldives.gov.mv> for information and news from the president's office.

<www.maldives.at/portal.html> for a listing of all websites promoting Maldives.

<www.fco.gov.uk> for the British Foreign Office travel advisory on the Maldives.

There is a cyber kiosk run by Dhiraagu, the telephone company, in the public concourse of Male' International Airport. Open 24 hours a day, charges are US$2 for 15 minutes, and US$5 for one hour. Privately run Internet café's exist throughout Male', and there is a convenient one at the Nasandhura Palace Hotel. The major resorts have dedicated business centres, while the smaller ones can help with sending/receiving emails. Some major resorts have broadband and wireless access available in the guest rooms.

Recommended Hotels

The Maldives has a variety of resorts to suit every holiday budget, ranging from 'all inclusive' at US$140 for two per night in a double room with all meals and drinks, to more than US$1,000 for two in a double room, without meals. The room rates reflect the resort's location, style and amenities, and are set to appeal to the kind of clientele the resort wants to attract.

Some resorts add a 10 percent service charge to their room rates, others don't, so it's worth asking about extras before confirming a reservation. The rates quoted here are for 2007 and subject to change. They are based on the lowest rate per night for a room for two with breakfast, except where stated.

The following abbreviations are used:

All All inclusive (room, meals and selected drinks for two)
HB Half board (room, breakfast and dinner for two)
FB Full board (room, breakfast, lunch and dinner for two)

$$$$$	US$1,000 and above
$$$$	$600–1,000
$$$	$300–600
$$	150–300
$	under $150

MALE'

Athama Palace $ *Dhivehi Ataa, Majeedhee Magu, tel: 331 3118, fax: 332 8828.* This is a pleasant, inexpensive place in the middle of town. Lots of stairs and small rooms, plus an Indian-style restaurant.

Burungee Residence $ *Hithahfinivaa Magu, tel: 333 0011, fax: 331 0022.* Comfortable, old-fashioned lounge and simply furnished rooms at a bargain price for Male' in a cosy garden setting.

Central $ *Sanoaraage, Rahdhebai Magu, tel: 331 7766, fax: 331 5383, <www.centralmaldives.com>.* A free shuttle service from the quayside makes it easier to find this hotel tucked down a side street in the centre of town. Rooms are smartly furnished although small; there is a lift and a top-floor restaurant.

Fresco $ *Dhon Bulhaage, Nasseemee Hingun, tel: 332 1146, fax: 334 0832, <www.hotelfresco.com>.* A new establishment of apartment units turned into guest rooms, some with shared bathrooms, on the western, residential part of town.

Hulhule Island Hotel $$ *Male' International Airport, tel: 333 0888, fax: 333 0777, <www.hih.com.mv>.* Ideal for business visitors since it has a free shuttle service to the capital, a lively pub, a coffee shop and à la carte restaurant, a swimming pool and city-style bedrooms with TV. It's usually fully booked with guests awaiting transfer to their resorts or flights home.

Kai Lodge $ *Mandhu Edhuruge, Violet Magu, tel: 332 8742, fax: 332 8738.* This guesthouse is located in a leafy compound down a quiet back street. It has the easy-going atmosphere of staying in a friend's place.

Kam Hotel $ *Roanuge, Meheli Goalhi, tel: 332 0611, fax: 332 0614.* With a small swimming pool, and near the airport jetty, the Kam is popular for overnighting. Rooms are elaborately furnished, giving it an up-market ambience.

Nasandhura Palace $ *Bodu Thakurufaanu Magu, tel: 333 8444, fax: 332 0822, <www.nasandhurapalace.com>.* The doyen of Male' hotels on the waterfront, but only two storeys high with most views blocked by extensions. It lies across the road from the airport jetty. Rooms are spacious and reception efficient. Ideal for business visitors. Its open-air Trends café is the place to be seen, and it has a cyber gallery too.

Relax Inn $ *Ameeru Ahmed Magu, tel: 331 4531, fax: 331 4533, <www.relaxmaldives.com>.* Behind the Nasandhura Palace at less cost, with small rooms and the Ground Six fast-food restaurant. Comfortable enough for a one-night transit stay.

Villingili View Inn $ *155 Majeedhee Magu, tel: 331 8696, fax: 332 5213, <www.tropicalisland.com.mv>* On the west coast with simple charm, a friendly place to stay, with a Maldivian atmosphere making it popular with locals too.

CRUISES

Atoll Explorer **$$ (FB)** *Universal Enterprises, Orchid Magu, Male', tel: 332 3080, fax: 332 2678, <www.atollexplorer.com>.* The ship makes one-week cruises through different atolls and has a diving school, a bar, a buffet restaurant and a lively, friendly atmosphere with crew joining in activities. There are never more than 40 passengers aboard. Cabins are compact; some have balconies.

NORTH MALE' ATOLL

Angsana $$$ *Ihuru Island, tel: 664 3502, fax: 664 5933, <www.angsana.com>.* An easy-going atmosphere in this fashionable resort (close to and associated with Banyan Tree) created on the pretty, round island of Ihuru. Even though the island is small, some areas are closed to protect the environment, in keeping with the concerns of its ecologically aware guests.

Asdu Sun Island $ (FB) *tel: 664 5051, fax: 664 0176, <www.asdu.com>.* Like the Maldives used to be, having only 30 rooms by the beach in blocks with ceilings of woven mats and coir rope. A vibrant house reef, and no TV, air-con or hot water, just a simple back-to-basics beachcomber ambience loved by guests who visit again and again, and get discounts for doing so. Even lower rates in May to June and October to November.

Bandos $ *tel: 664 0088, fax: 664 3877, <www.bandos.com>.* A firm favourite of regulars since it opened in 1973. Recently remodelled with thatched, beehive-roofed cottages and a couple of overwater villas, this island near Male' can accommodate 450 and has the facilities (tennis, badminton, squash, aerobics, spa, gym, etc.) to keep guests happy on land as well as under the water. Five restaurants and bars. Open to non-residents too.

Banyan Tree $$$$ *Vabbinfaru, tel: 664 3147, fax: 664 3843, <www.banyantree.com>.* Intimate in a five-star manner with special design touches and gourmet menus, this island has good beaches and vegetation. The 48 rooms are built as thatched-roof cottages opening on all sides to the beach and furnished with four-poster beds. The emphasis is on a low-key, tranquil experience.

Baros Maldives $$$ *tel: 664 2672, fax: 664 3497, <www. baros.com>.* For years Baros was popular for a reliable tropical-island holiday. Now completely rebuilt, it has spacious, wood themed cottages with TV concealed in the foot-of-bed ottoman, a mini wine cellar and minibar, and a garden bathroom with bathtub and rain shower. The 30 overwater villas have private sun decks and bathrooms with lagoon view. With central palm-garden bar, a seafood grill and a great gourmet restaurant (Lighthouse), this small island still provides all that's expected of a tropical paradise.

Four Seasons Kudu Huraa $$$$ *tel: 664 4888, fax: 664 4800, <www.fourseasons.com>.* Reopened after being severely damaged by the tsunami, this resort stretches a long distance from its over-water villas at one end to its infinity swimming pool and restaurants at the other. Some beach villas have their own swimming pools and are lavishly decorated with timber and thatch. Fine fusion cuisine and caring service.

Full Moon Maldives $$ *Furana, tel: 664 2010, fax: 664 1979, <www.fullmoonmaldives.com>.* All-new accommodation on this recently rebuilt, well-established resort run with professionalism, only 20 minutes by speedboat from Male'. Over-lagoon thatched-roof lodges line one side of this long island, with beachfront cottages in crescents on the other side, plus rooms in 10 four-unit mansions and five offshore water villas. A spa on its own island reached by a boardwalk, a free-form swimming pool, spacious deck bar and superb restaurants are added attractions.

Giraavaru $ (FB) *tel: 664 0440, fax: 664 4818, <www.giravaru.com>*. A small resort into which are squeezed 66 rooms in blocks, Giraavaru has long attracted young, independent budget travellers and is a fine introduction to the beaches and reefs of the Maldives. Meals are buffets, rooms are basic and the atmosphere free and easy. Only 50 minutes by *dhoni* (25 by speedboat) from Male', this is an option for first-timers who just want sea, sun and fun.

Hudhuranfushi $$ *tel: 334 3867, fax: 332 5237, <www. adaaran.com>*. Formerly Lohifushi and a favourite with surfers, this is a large island with a coconut plantation and 137 upgraded beach villas and 40 offshore water villas. There are bars at both ends, one with a view of the surf.

Huvafenfushi $$$$ *tel: 664 4222, fax: 664 4333, <www.huvafenfushi.com>*. Famous for the first-ever underwater spa, this resort caters for the international set. Its 43 timber beach, lagoon and water cottages, each with private plunge pool, are fitted out in designer luxury. An underground wine cellar doubles as a private dining room, the bar is retro-tiled, and there is a sense of guests being trendsetters when staying at this small, pretty island.

Kurumba Maldives $$$ *tel: 664 2324, fax: 664 3885, <www.kurumba.com>*. A legend in the Maldives as the resort where tourism began, Kurumba has undergone many metamorphoses to retain its position as the first resort in every sense. This is grand hotel style for the discerning, with 20 hectares (48 acres) criss-crossed with flower-bedecked paths giving access to accommodation designed for privacy. Classically moulded high walls surround individual swimming pools, secluded garden bathrooms and villas opening on to sun decks by the beach. With a sports centre, a water-themed spa and enough restaurants for a week of dining differently every night, the resort is dedicated to satisfying guests whether staying on business or holiday.

Paradise Island $$ (FB) *tel: 664 0011, fax: 664 0022, <www.villahotels.com>*. Big-city ambience livens up this long island, which has 220 rooms and 40 semi-detached villas over the lagoon, and lots of things to do on land as well as over and under the water. Popular, not just because it's only 20 minutes from the airport, but also for its action-packed holiday product.

Soneva Gili $$$$$ *tel: 664 0304, fax: 664 0305 <www.sixsenses. com>*. No breakfast included in the room rate, but the rooms are amazing. Built of timber and thatch and furnished like luxury log cabins, all are over water, some reached only by rowing boat. The smallest is 210 sq m (2,260 sq ft), all have two wings, two levels and absolute privacy. The cuisine is as select as the guests, and it's only 15 minutes from the airport.

SOUTH MALE' ATOLL

Anantara Maldives $$$ *Dhigufinholu, tel: 664 4100, fax: 664 4101, <www.anantara.com>*. With a design that introduces Thai touches to its Maldivian architecture (such as hanging canopies, plump cushions and lashings of silk), Anantara revels in its stylish combination of tropical fantasy and the latest gadgetry (there's an iPod docking station in every room). There are 38 spacious teak-furnished over-water suites and 68 roomy beach-front villas, plus four pool suites on this 2-hectare (5-acre) island. Other features are an over-water spa complex and a range of restaurants, including a Thai one reached by boat. Exotically clad staff, fusion cookery classes and a swimming pool that sparkles at night add individuality to this top-end resort.

Club Rannalhi $$ (FB) *tel: 664 2688, fax: 664 2035, <www. adaaran.com>*. This resort appeals to the energetic who like organised activities and comfortable rooms, whether in two-storey chalets on the beach or over the water.

Embudu Village $ (FB) *tel: 664 4776, fax: 664 2673, <www. embudu.com>*. A small, compact island with ample shade and vegetation; more than 100 rooms and 16 water villas with glass viewing panels in the floor. The sand-floored lobbies set the theme of rustic simplicity of this resort, a great favourite with repeaters for a good-value holiday.

Laguna Maldives $$ *Velassaru, tel: 664 3042, fax: 664 3041,
<www.lagunamaldives.com>*. Part of the Maldivian-owned Uni-
versal Resorts group, Laguna is a neat resort with attractively des-
igned rooms and elegant over-water suites. With four restaurants,
charming service and modern amenities, it is popular because of its
consistent and affordable quality.

Taj Exotica $$$$ *tel: 664 2200, fax: 664 2211, <www.tajhotels.
com>*. As part of the Taj Hotels group of India, this resort reflects
the standards of its parent, adapted to a tropical island environment.
It was closed as a result of the tsunami and emerged revamped with
62 villas, most grouped in a horseshoe shape offshore and the rest
on the beach.

Vadoo $$ (FB) *tel: 664 3976, fax: 664 3397, <www.vadoo.net>*.
Long a favourite with divers, many from Japan, this island is so
small it takes only a few minutes to explore. A friendly resort,
although not much partying as most guests are there for the diving.

ARI AND RASDHOO ATOLLS

Bathala $$ (FB) *tel: 668 0587, fax: 668 0558, <www.adaaran.
com>*. On the eastern edge of Ari Atoll, Bathala is small and infor-
mal in the original manner of the Maldives, with rustic cottages and
fairly basic facilities, hugely popular with divers and repeat guests.

Dhoni Mighili $$$$$ (All) *tel: 666 0751, fax: 666 0727, <www.
dhonimighili.com>*. Accommodation is in one of six *dhonis*, with
luxury bungalow accommodation nestling in the palm trees for
nights ashore. One of the highest-priced resorts in the Maldives, this
is nevertheless low key and unpretentious, giving a sense of inti-
macy where guests can delight in sun, sand and sea at their own
pace. No children are allowed.

Ellaidoo $ (HB) *tel: 666 0586, fax: 666 0514, <www.travelin-
maldives.com>*. Sharing the eastern rim with Bathala, this resort
appeals to the diving community, most of whom come from Ger-
many and Austria. Avenues of coconut palms and thick vegetation

shade 78 basic-structure chalets and room blocks built around the island's edge. Meals are buffets and there is a coffee shop and bar, as well as a fascinating house reef.

Hilton $$$ *Rangali Island, tel: 668 0629, fax: 668 0619 <www. maldives.hilton.com>.* With its underwater restaurant for 12 and a chance to bump into celebrities, staying at this resort has cachet, as well as long walks on the wooden bridge linking its two islands and over-water villas; there are beach villas too. The accommodation is classy with matching courteous service and sophisticated ambience. Although there is good diving, guests seem to prefer being spoilt on land.

Holiday Island $$ (FB) *Dhiffushi, tel 668 0011, fax: 668 0022, <www.villahotels.com>.* A resort popular for a good family holiday in the manner of the local Villa Hotels group, which operates it. Lots of entertainment, buffets, and smart, modern chalet accommodation. Guests are mostly from Germany, Italy and Switzerland.

Kuramathi Blue Lagoon $$ *tel: 666 0527, fax: 666 0556, <www.kuramathi.com.mv>.* Kuramathi is unique in the Maldives as it consists of three resorts on one large island, 1.6km (1 mile) long and 550m (600yds) at its widest. This not only gives lots of wilderness to explore but also the chance to eat in a different resort restaurant every night. Blue Lagoon has a combination of over-water cabanas of timber, and beach bungalows in flower gardens. At the opposite end of the island to Kuramathi village, its bar deck is popular for sundowners and watching manta rays.

Kuramathi Cottage $$ *tel: 666 0527, fax: 666 0556, <www. kuramathi.com.mv>.* In the middle of Kuramathi, it has water and beach cottages and a more exclusive ambience than its neighbours. Its Thai restaurant is deservedly popular.

Kuramathi Village $$ (HB) *tel: 666 0527, fax: 666 0556, <www.kuramathi.com.mv>.* While all three Kuramathi resorts are enjoyable, Village has long been known for the fun to be had in its informal environment with guests from around the world seeking good-quality, standard accommodation by a beach. There is an Indian speciality restaurant and a bar famed for its camaraderie.

Nika Island $$$$ (FB) *Kudafolhudhoo, tel: 666 0516, fax: 666 0577, <www.nikamaldive.com>.* With accommodation in 26 cottages with sitting room and bedroom, each built in its own low-walled garden in a village setting, Nika has long been favoured for its traditional hospitality and exclusivity.

Sun Island $$ (FB) *Nalaguraidhoo, tel: 668 0088, fax: 668 0099, <www.villahotels.com>.* Another Villa Hotels resort featuring the group's hallmark of good value and good fun. A large island with broad beaches and accommodation for 700 guests on land and over water. There are 10 bars and Thai, Japanese and Italian restaurants and a jolly atmosphere appealing to all nationalities.

White Sands $$ (HB) *tel: 668 0513, fax: 668 0512, <www. maldiveswhitesands.com>.* Not so large as its neighbours, Sun and Holiday islands, this nevertheless shares the party ambience with lots of restaurants, bars and entertainment. Accommodation is in Maldivian-style houseboats over the lagoon or on the beach.

W Retreat & Spa $$$$ *Fesdu, tel: 666 2222, fax: 666 2200, <www.whotels.com>.* A concept based on 'ultra chic lifestyle' has transformed the once rustic 4-hectare (10-acre) island of Fesdu into a slick resort. With 78 over-water and beach-side rooms (called 'retreats'), all with plunge pools and six places to dine and drink (including an underground vodka bar), a private over-water spa, and international staff ever at hand, guests may find it hard to believe they are on an island.

BAA ATOLL

Coco Palm $$$ *Dhunikolhu, tel: 660 0011, fax: 660 0022, <www. cococollection.com.mv>.* Romance is the theme with champagne breakfasts and sunset cocktails on this large island, which has beach and lagoon villas lavishly finished with wood, rattan and cotton. The beaches are stunning and the snorkelling good.

Four Seasons Landaa Giraavaru $$$$ *tel: 660 0888, fax: 660 0800, <www.fourseasons.com>*. This large (18-hectare/44-acre) resort is a natural wonder, with its western tip of white sand sloping into a 2-km (1¼-mile) long lagoon. Accommodation combines land and sea, with a beach pavilion living area linked by wooden walkway to an over-sea sleeping pavilion. Contemporary cuisine is offered and there are Italian and Arabic speciality restaurants.

Reethi Beach $ *tel: 660 2626, fax: 660 2727, <www.reethibeach. com.mv>*. Surprisingly in a new resort, accommodation is modestly priced, so this one appeals to the young and active who like the simple practicality of the 70 rooms and 30 over-water bungalows. There is a Chinese restaurant supplementing the main restaurant buffets, and lots of water sports too.

Royal Island $$ *Horubadhoo, tel: 660 0088, fax: 660 0099, <www.villahotels.com>*. Newer and more up-market than other Villa Hotels' resorts, this one consists of 148 beach villas and two suites in a long island with dense vegetation including large banyan trees. Wood is used extensively in the furnishings, which are complemented with modern amenities like email access. There are sports and water activities, and a herbal spa.

Soneva Fushi $$$$ *Kunfunadhoo, tel: 660 0304, fax: 660 0374, <www.sixsenses.com>*. This trendsetting resort has extravagantly designed individual villas built in the wilderness. Coir, coral and clay are used for the fittings and everything is eco-oriented. Wonderful for walks, beach privacy and indulging in island fantasy, sustained with gourmet fare and good company.

RAA ATOLL

Adaaran Water Villas $$$$ *tel: 658 0125, fax: 658 0127, <www. thewatervillas.com>*. Part of the Meedhupparu resort, Adaaran consists of 20 over-water villas in the lagoon off the jungly shore. Each has teak furnishing and a sun deck with Jacuzzi, a day bed and a glass panel to view the lagoon below. There is a restaurant and bar, and guests have the run of Meedhupparu and its facilities.

Meedhupparu $$ *tel: 658 7700, fax: 658 5500, <www.adaaran. com> and <www.meedhuparru.com>*. Lots to do (there's even a hairdresser) on this resort set alone in Raa Atoll. Accommodation for over 400 guests is in smart units on part of this large (17-hectare/43-acre) island, which has great beaches and lagoon. If life gets a bit too hectic, there is also an **Ayurveda Village** (*<www. ayurvedamaldives.com>*) in a self-contained private section of the island with its own restaurant for guests who wish to have the Sri Lankan herbal therapy of ayurveda.

LHAVIYANI ATOLL

Komandoo $$ (FB) *tel: 662 1010, fax: 662 1011, <www. komandoo.com>*. Only 45 beach-front rooms, built using timber inside and out, with modern facilities and deep verandas. With a shallow lagoon and nearby house reef, the resort has a tranquil atmosphere, ideal for a lazy holiday.

Kuredu $ (HB) *tel: 662 0337, fax: 662 0332, <www.kuredu.com>*. Popular with the young of all ages and with all nationalities, Kuredu has mass-market appeal. Endless beaches, five restaurants, plenty of bars, lots to do (including golf), with basic and luxury beach or over-water villa accommodation for 660 guests.

One & Only Kanuhura $$$$ *tel: 662 0044, fax: 662 0033, <www.oneandonlykanuhura.com.mv>*. One hundred luxurious beach and water villas set on this long island with soft white-sand beaches and good diving. Four restaurants, two bars and a spa for the discerning, with a kids' club to keep families happy.

HAA ALIF ATOLL

Island Hideaway Marina & Spa $$$$ *Dhonakulhi, tel: 650 1515, fax: 650 1616, <www.island-hideaway.com>*. It's a long way to go (with a 45-minute domestic flight and a 15-minute speedboat ride), but to arrive at Island Hideaway is to discover a unique get-away. The island is long and covered in jungle, with so many paths (bicycles and buggies are available) it's easy to get lost. Each large, thatched, beach-side villa is set in a private glade and – with private pool, roof garden sun deck and in-villa dining on demand served by a butler – guests can keep to themselves, or venture out to the over-water spa and fine dining restaurants. With over 200 staff for 43 villas, attention to guests' needs is guaranteed.

FAAFU ATOLL

Rania Experience $$$$$ (All) *tel: 674 0555, <www.rania experience.com>.* The Rania Experience is based on absolute exclusivity for just two people, with a private 26-m (86-ft) yacht available for cruising and an entire island, The Water Garden Island Spa, in this undeveloped atoll. Diving and spa therapy, and practically everything else, is included in the cost of US$12,000 per night for two, three night-minimum stay.

MEEMU ATOLL

Hakura Club $$ (All) *tel: 672 0014, fax: 672 0013, <www. chaayahotels.com>* and *<www.johnkeellshotels.com>.* Located in one of the longest stretches of reefs in the Maldives, Hakura Club is unique in design, with gleaming, pinnacled white roofs defining its 70 rooms, which are built offshore along the island's length. The restaurant, bar and public areas are on the 2.5-hectare (6-acre) island where there are also 10 beach rooms. Lots of activities, including daily *dhoni* trips for snorkelling. Popular with British guests on all-inclusive packages.

ADDU ATOLL

Equator Village $ (All) *Gan, tel: 689 8721, fax: 689 8020, <www.equatorvillage.com>.* Equator Village offers a different Maldives holiday since it is possible to ride a bicycle or hire a taxi to tour the villages linked to Gan by causeway, or walk to the bank, post office and local shopping complex near Gan airport. Accommodation is less elaborate than at other island resorts, being simple chalets. The beaches are poor, but there's a swimming pool and organised diving to a war-time shipwreck, *British Loyalty.*

Recommended Restaurants

Tourists on an excursion from a resort do not usually dine in Male', but a visit to the capital is a good opportunity to pop into any typical tea shop to sample Maldivian snacks. There are only a few restaurants. The price for lunch or dinner at those listed here is from US$4 to $8 for a main course, no alcohol served.

To dine at a resort when visiting from elsewhere, reservations should be made, so that jetty security knows about your visit in advance. At the resorts, dinner is from US$50, wine from US$20 a bottle. The resorts listed here are within a 25-minute speedboat ride from each other, and from Male', and the boat charter cost has to be added to the price for a great evening out.

MALE' RESTAURANTS

Café Alfresco *Trade Centre Building, Orchid Magu, tel: 333 3084.* In the well of the STO shopping atrium, with a nautical look, this café is always busy with snacking shoppers and local people-watchers.

Fish Market Café *Bodu Thakurufaanu Magu.* On the first floor above the tiled area where freshly caught fish is gutted and sold, this noisy café is the haunt of fisherfolk, vendors and locals-in-the-know who want cheap tea, snacks and generous portions for lunch or dinner with a real Maldivian flavour. Not for the fastidious.

Galanga Café *Sosun Magu.* Hidden behind a small door set in the wall is this sand-floored garden café with rooftop patio and a view of the back yards of neighbouring houses. All-day snacks, lunch and dinner from a limited menu served swiftly in a relaxing ambience.

Kam Hotel *Roanuge, Meheli Goalhi, tel: 332 0611.* At the end of the lane alongside the Nasandhura Palace Hotel leading from the jetty, the Kam Hotel has a top-floor restaurant that is ideal for a quiet, Western-style dinner in a sophisticated setting with harbour views.

Lighthouse *Lily Magu, tel: 331 0900*. Upstairs restaurant in the road behind the old mosque in Sultan's Park featuring an innovative menu. Open for lunch, but reservations are needed for dinner.

Queen of the Night *Bodu Thakurufaanu Magu, tel: 332 2653*. Opposite the taxi rank by the jetty for airport *dhonis*, this café is always packed with Maldivians enjoying tea, short eats and rice and fish for lunch and dinner. Great for an authentic Maldivian breakfast of *mas huni* (shredded tuna) and *roshi* (griddle-made bread).

Raaveriya *155 Majeedhee Magu, tel: 331 8696*. In the patio garden and upstairs at Villingili View Inn on the west coast, this restaurant has a rural ambience and basic dishes. Open for lunch and dinner, with patio dining pleasant at night.

Royal Garden Café *Medhuziyaraiy Magu, tel: 332 0822*. In the old Esjehi Villa by Sultan's Park, with ancient wooden panelling (step into the air-conditioned interior for a look around) and a small garden, ideal for a coffee break or a snack.

Salsa Café *Keneri Magu, tel: 331 0319*. Behind a compound wall there is an open-air sand-floored veranda café and stairs to the upper restaurant deck. Open all day with an international menu.

Salsa Royal *Orchid Magu, tel: 333 5008*. More up-market than its sister establishment, Salsa Café, this is a smart place with prices to match for well-prepared European and Asian cuisine. Usually occupied by groups at lunch time, so probably better for dinner.

Seagull Café *Fareedhee Magu, tel: 332 3332*. On the corner where the road joins Chandhanee Magu, this sand-floored garden café and ice-cream parlour has long been popular with visitors, as well as locals.

South Café *South Breeze, Bodu Thakurufaanu Magu, tel: 334 0951*. In the residential, south-east section of Male', this café serving low-cost local dishes is usually packed with Maldivian and foreign workers enjoying a quick snack or meal in a noisy atmosphere.

Thai Wok *Ameer Ahmed Magu, tel: 331 0007*. A hit since it opened. Basic décor with sensational Thai food; open for lunch and dinner, reservation essential.

Trends *Nasandhura Palace Hotel, Bodu Thakurufaanu Magu, tel: 332 3380. The* meeting place throughout the day, from breakfast buffet to special-theme evening dinners. There's a comprehensive menu.

RESORT DINING

Bandos *tel: 332 5529*. The **Harbour Restaurant** features Maldivian fish dishes and grilled meats, while the **Sand Bar** pub is usually lively (think airline crews on long layovers).

Baros Maldives *tel: 664 2672*. Another treat for foodies. If you can get a reservation at the Lighthouse you will have a chance to try tantalising *degustation* menus, wines included, or individual fusion-inspired dishes. The chefs at the Cayenne Grill prepare seafood or meats exactly as you demand.

Full Moon Maldives *tel: 332 3080*. The Atoll Grill overlooks the lagoon and specialises in seafood and grilled items. Baan Thai serves Thai food, while Casa Luna has Mediterranean cuisine.

Hulhule Island Hotel *tel: 333 0888*. The traditional Euro-décor Captain's Fun Pub is popular with foreigners based in Male' as it is the closest place for a drink. The Gaidhoo Grill specialises in seafood and the adjoining Faru Coffee House serves European, Japanese and Italian dishes. There is a free boat shuttle service from Male'.

Kurumba Maldives *tel: 664 2324*. With the broadest selection of good restaurants of any resort in the Maldives, it is worth staying at Kurumba for the food alone. Its star for dinner is the Ocean Grill, entered by bridge over a lobster pool where your dinner swims. The Hamakaze is an informal sushi bar and *teppanyaki* outlet. Formal dining for gourmets is presented at the Golden Cowrie. The Al Qasr is an Arabian restaurant, while Ming Court serves splendid Chinese food. Next door is Kurumba Mahal for traditional Indian dishes.

INDEX